Street Art:
A Coloring Book

This book is dedicated John, my partner in life and love. Thank you for supporting my dreams. And to my dog, Tino—my constant companion, friend, and protector.

Photography curated from the Public Domain through Unsplashed and Pixabay.

Copyright © 2018 Mary Berrios Liuzzi

All rights reserved.

ISBN:1721225277

ISBN-13:978-1721225279

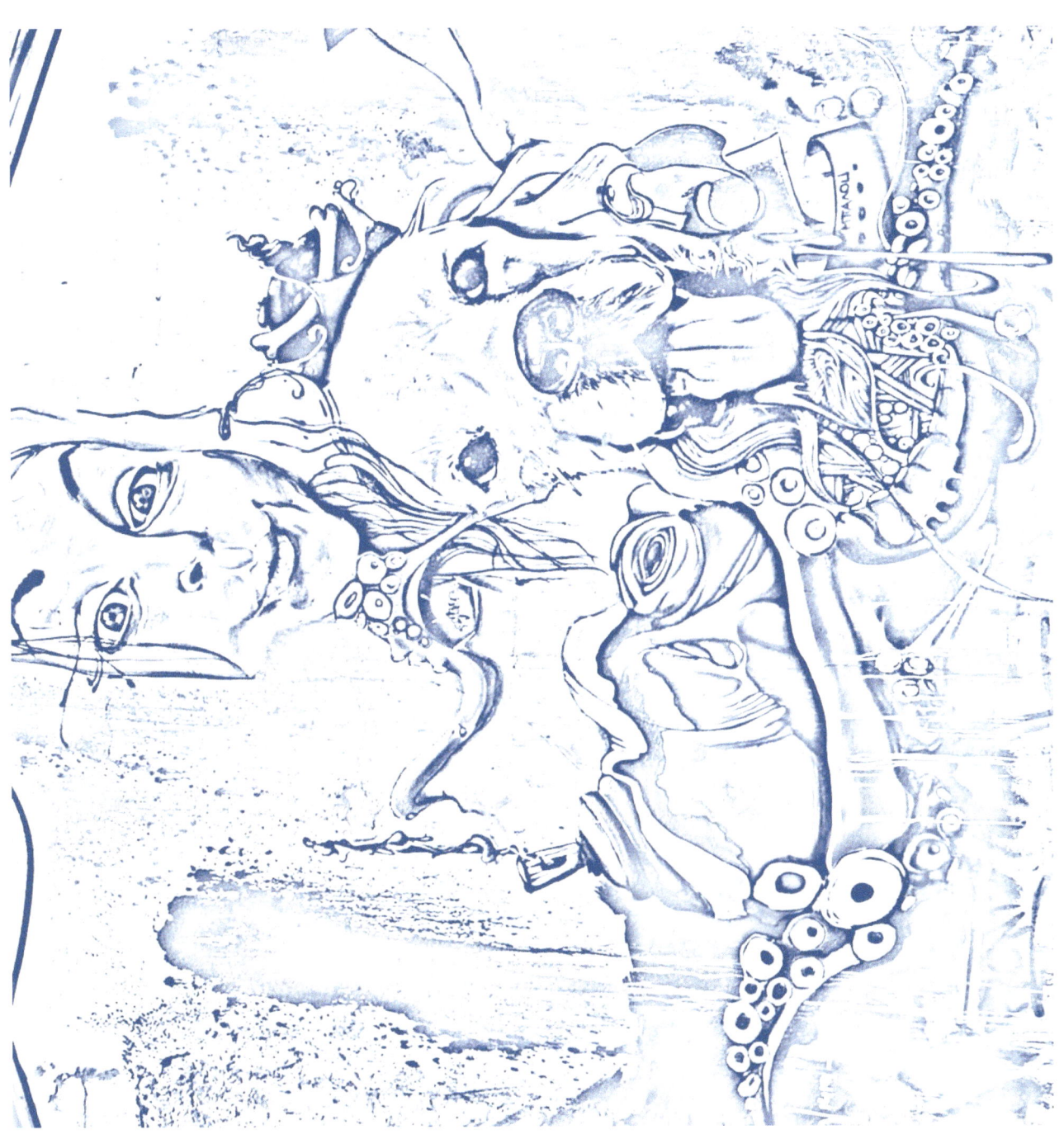

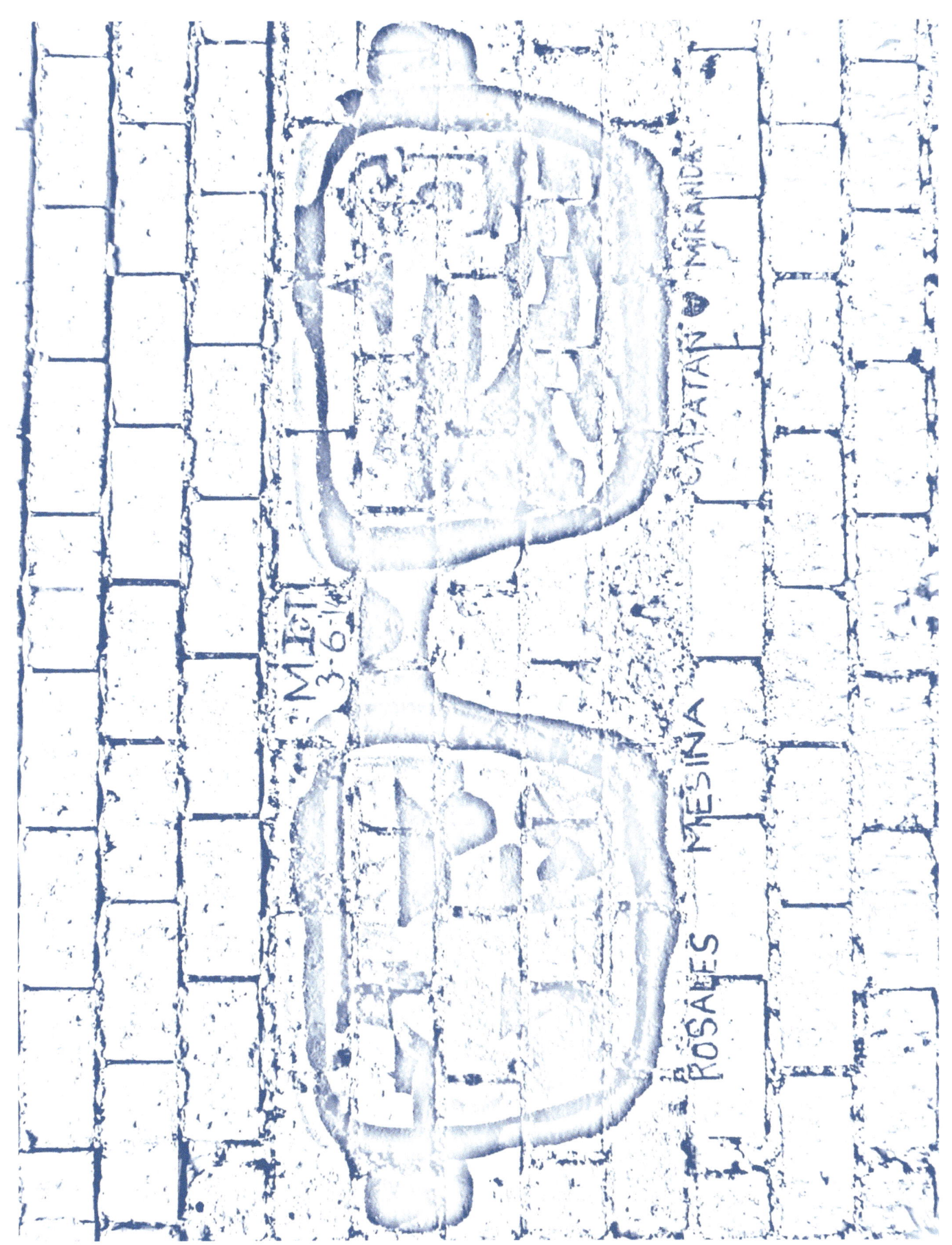

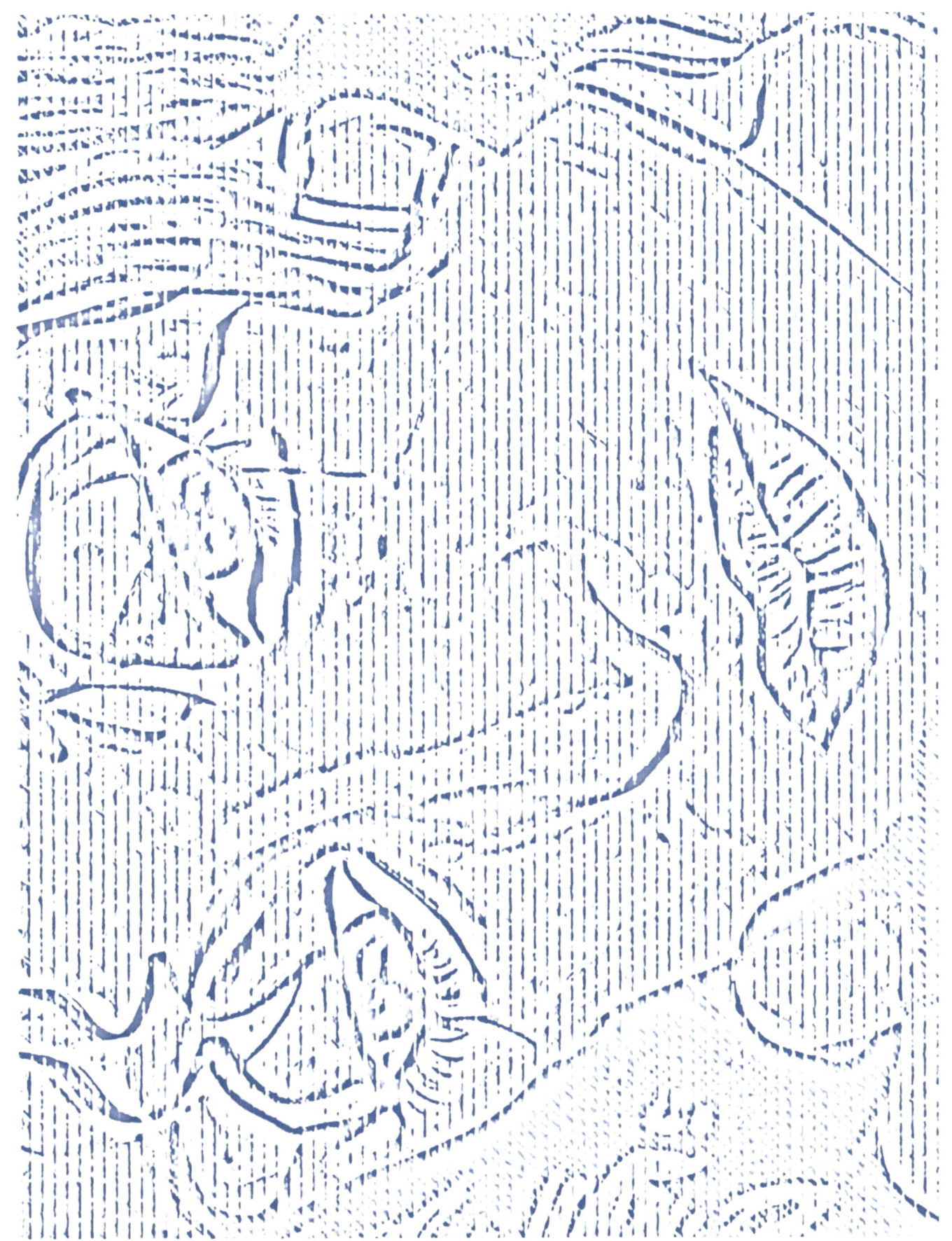

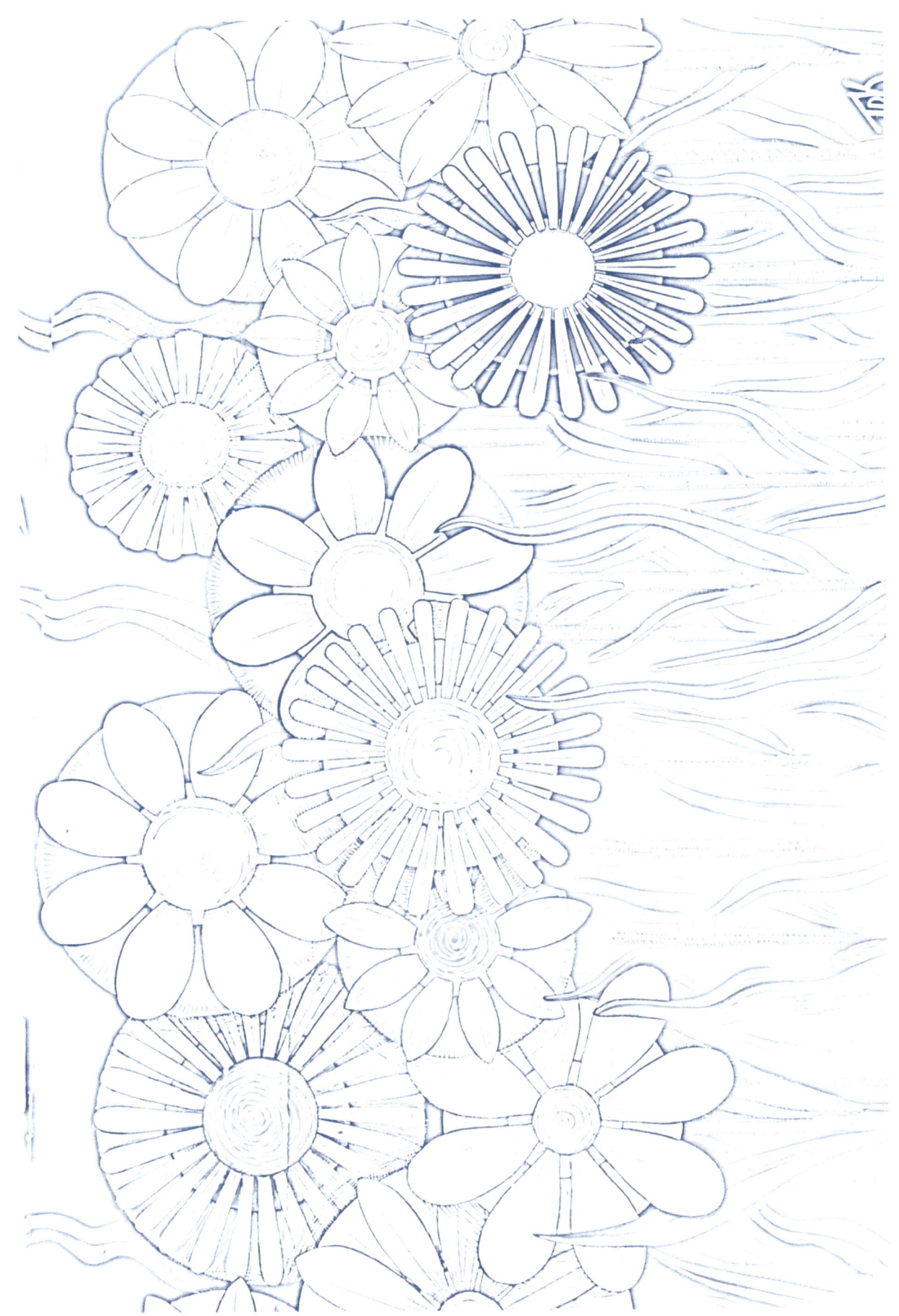

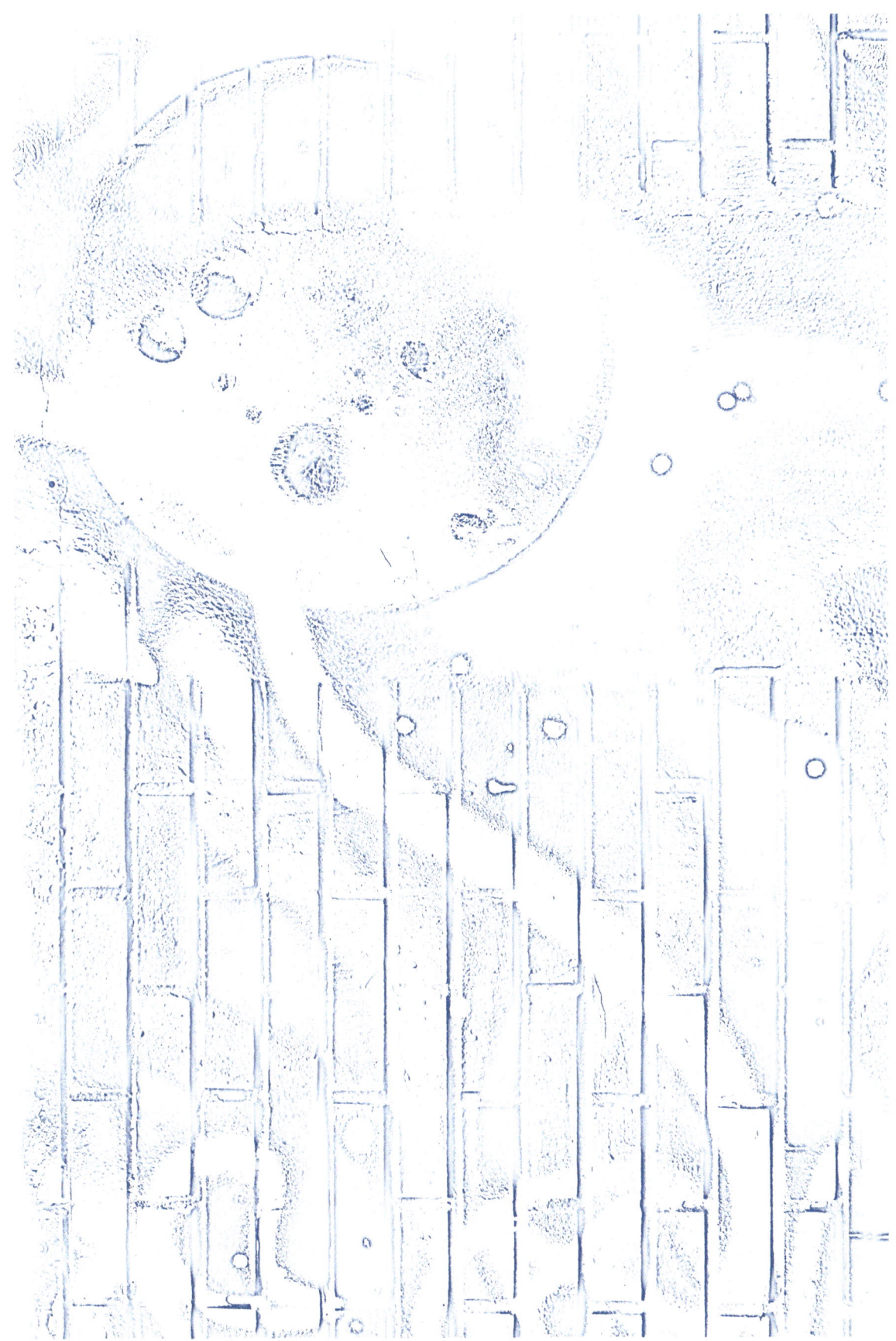

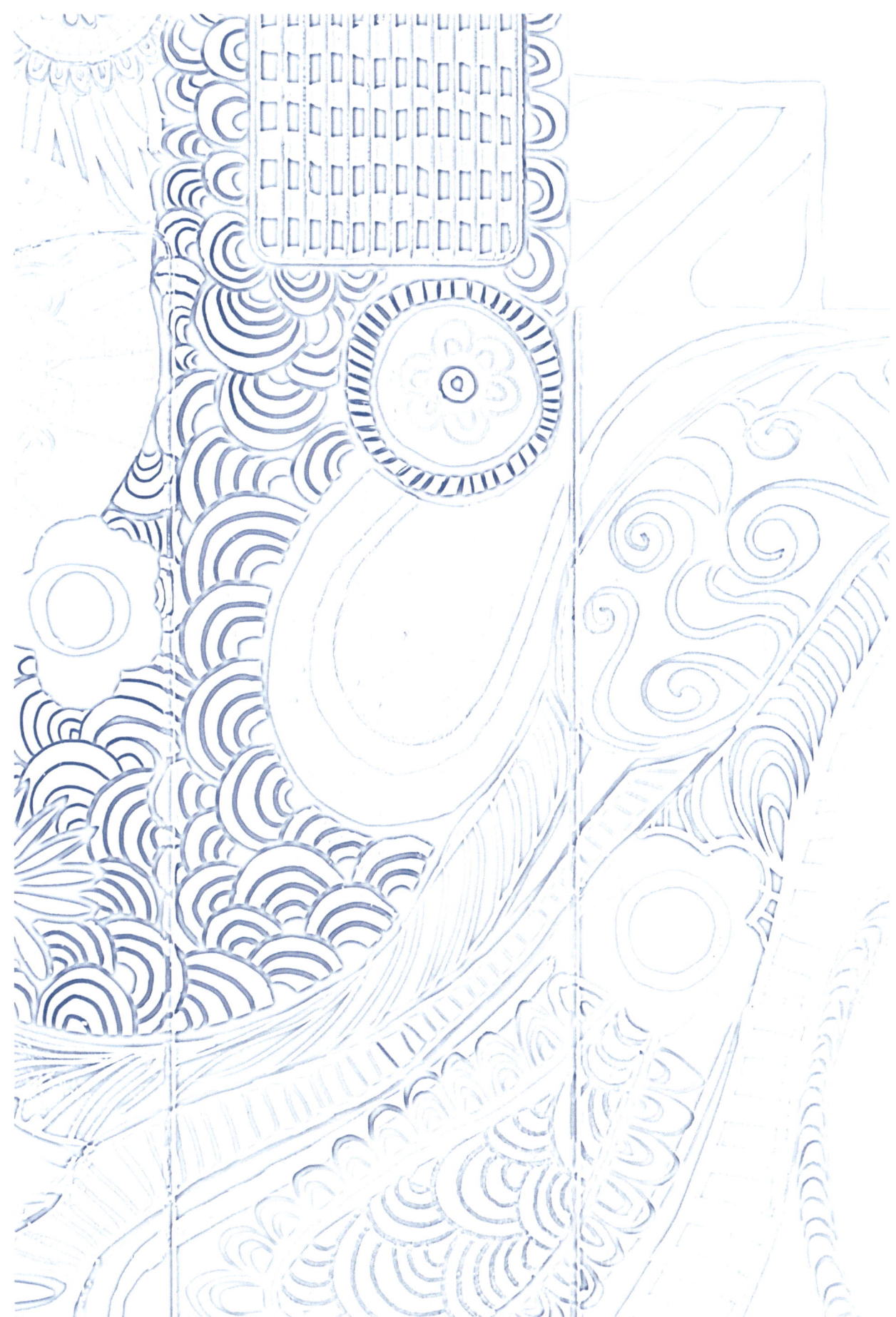

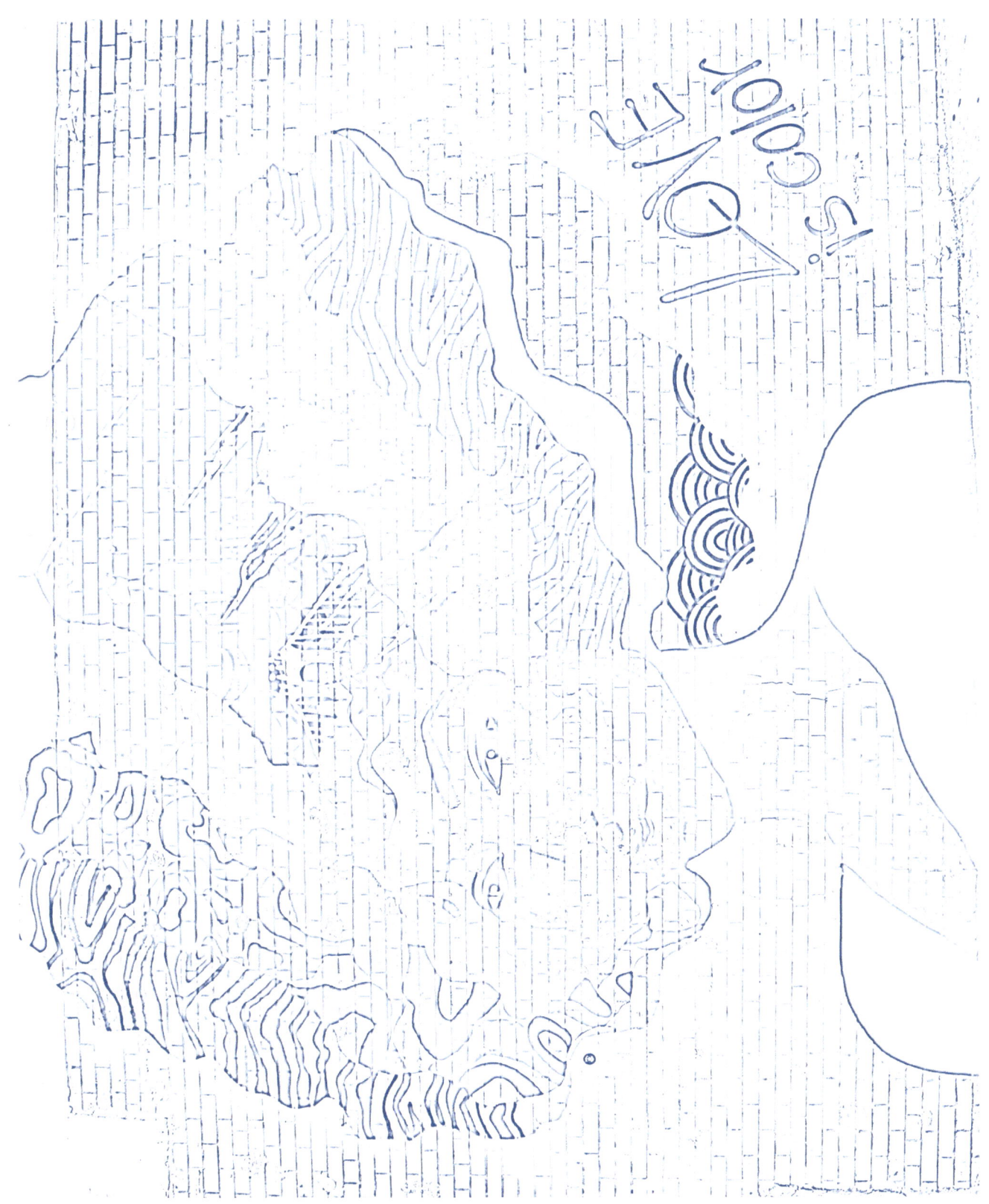

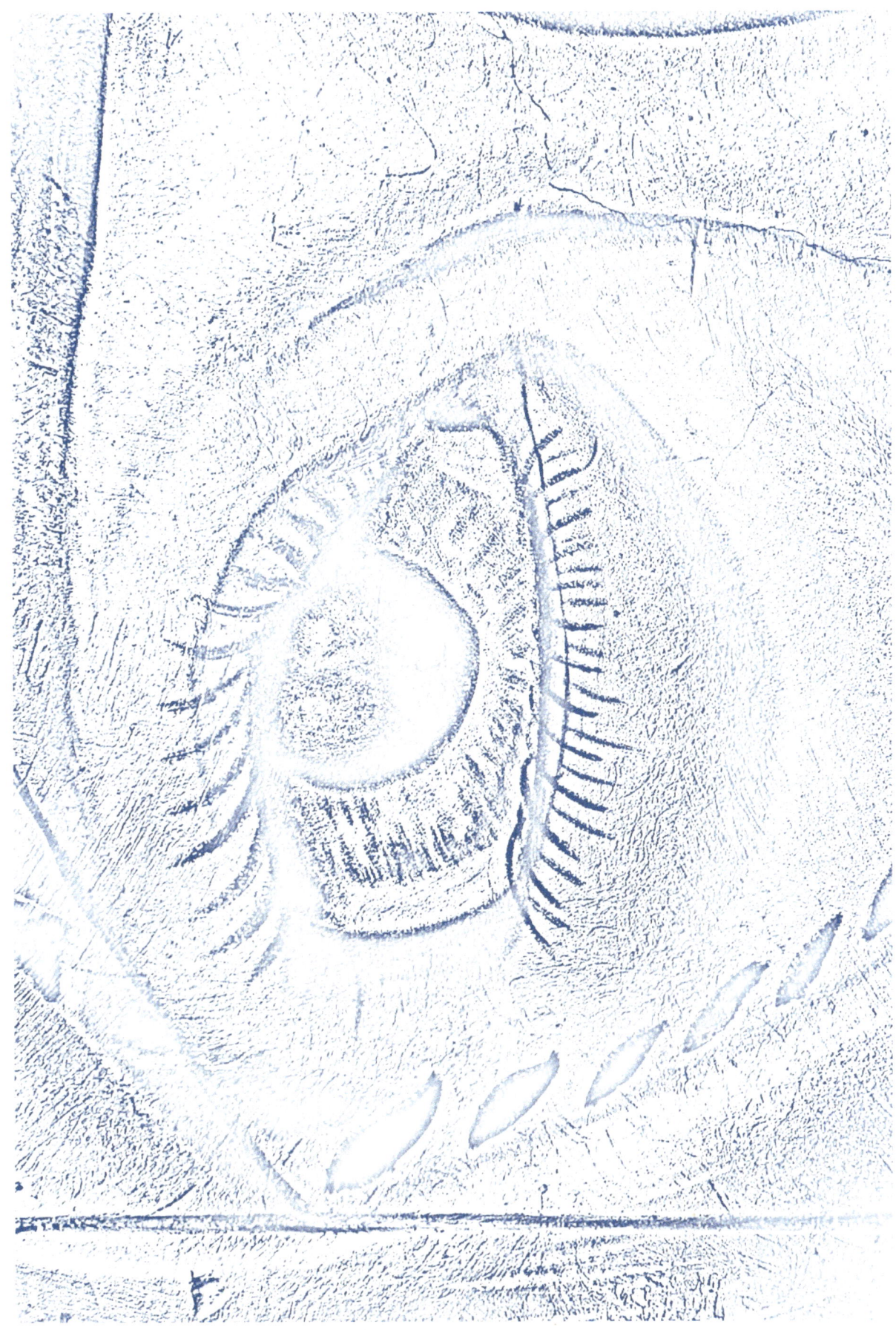

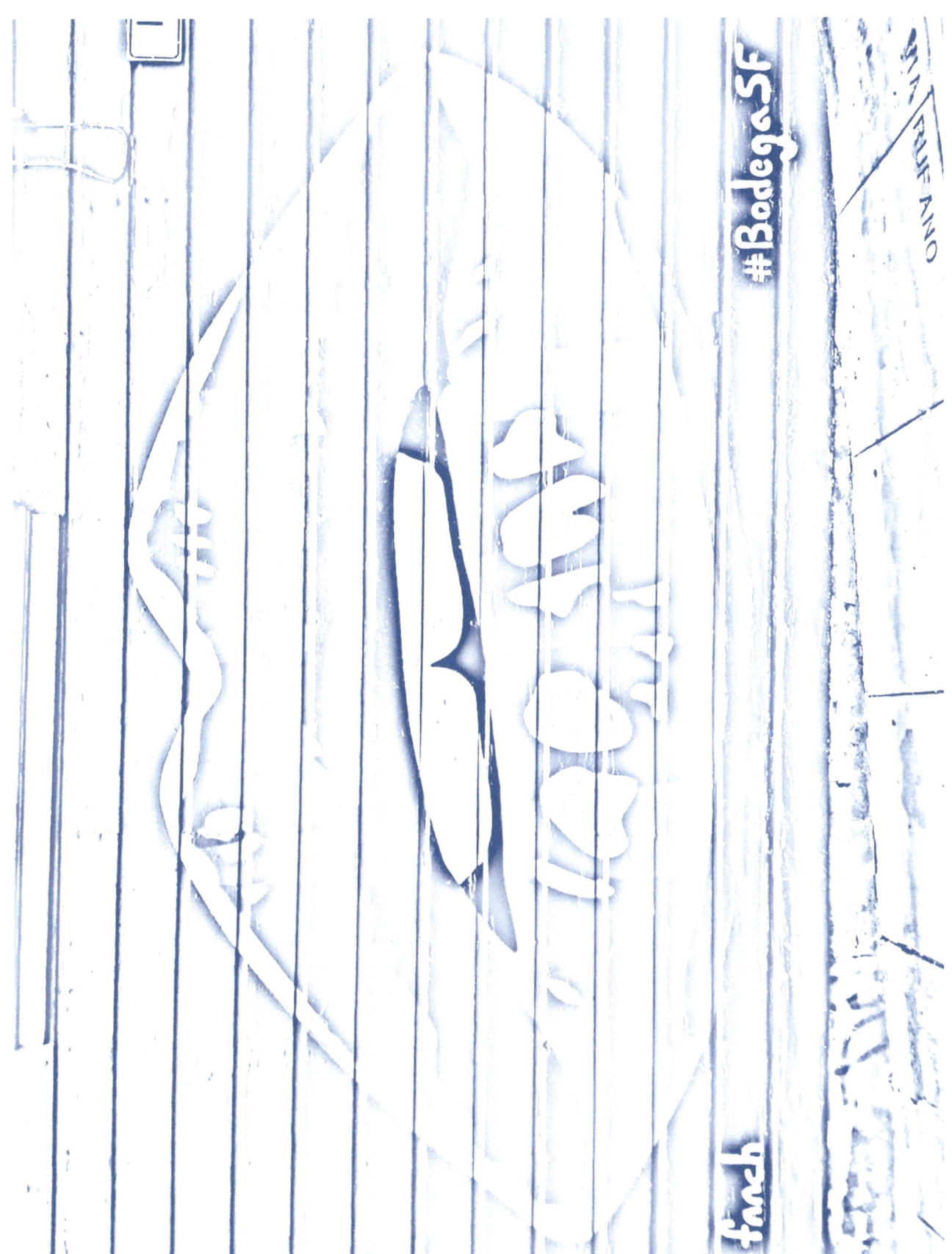

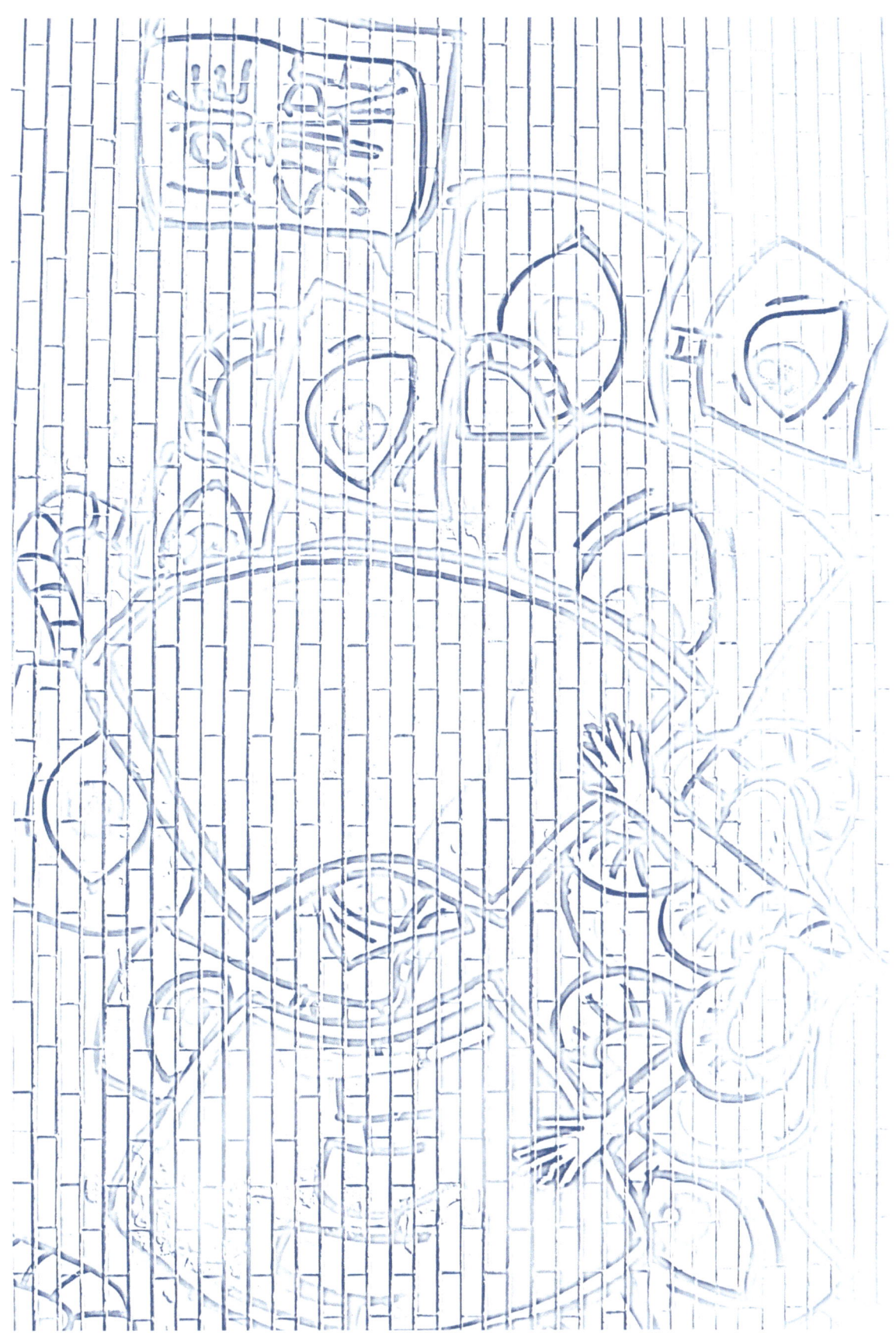

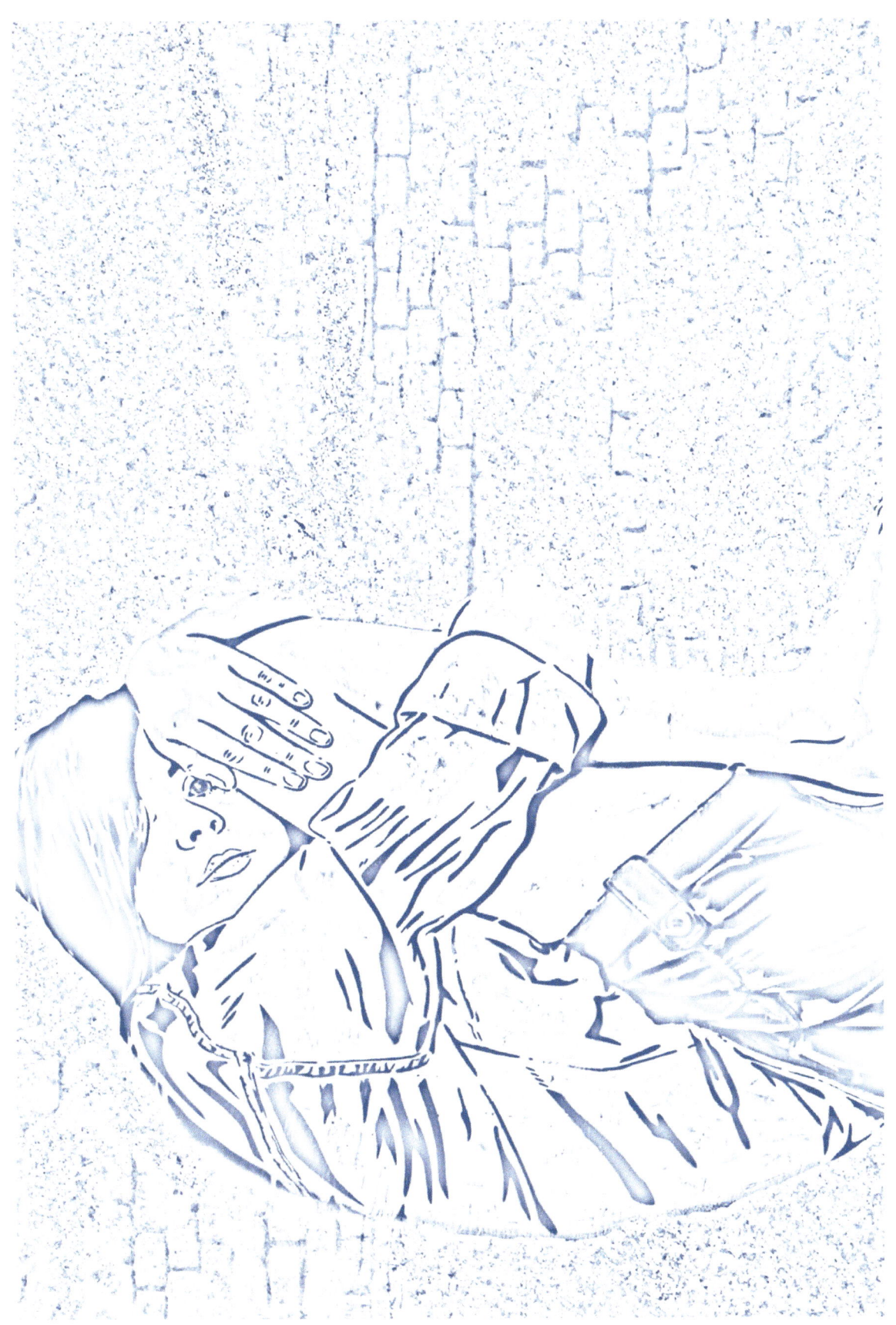

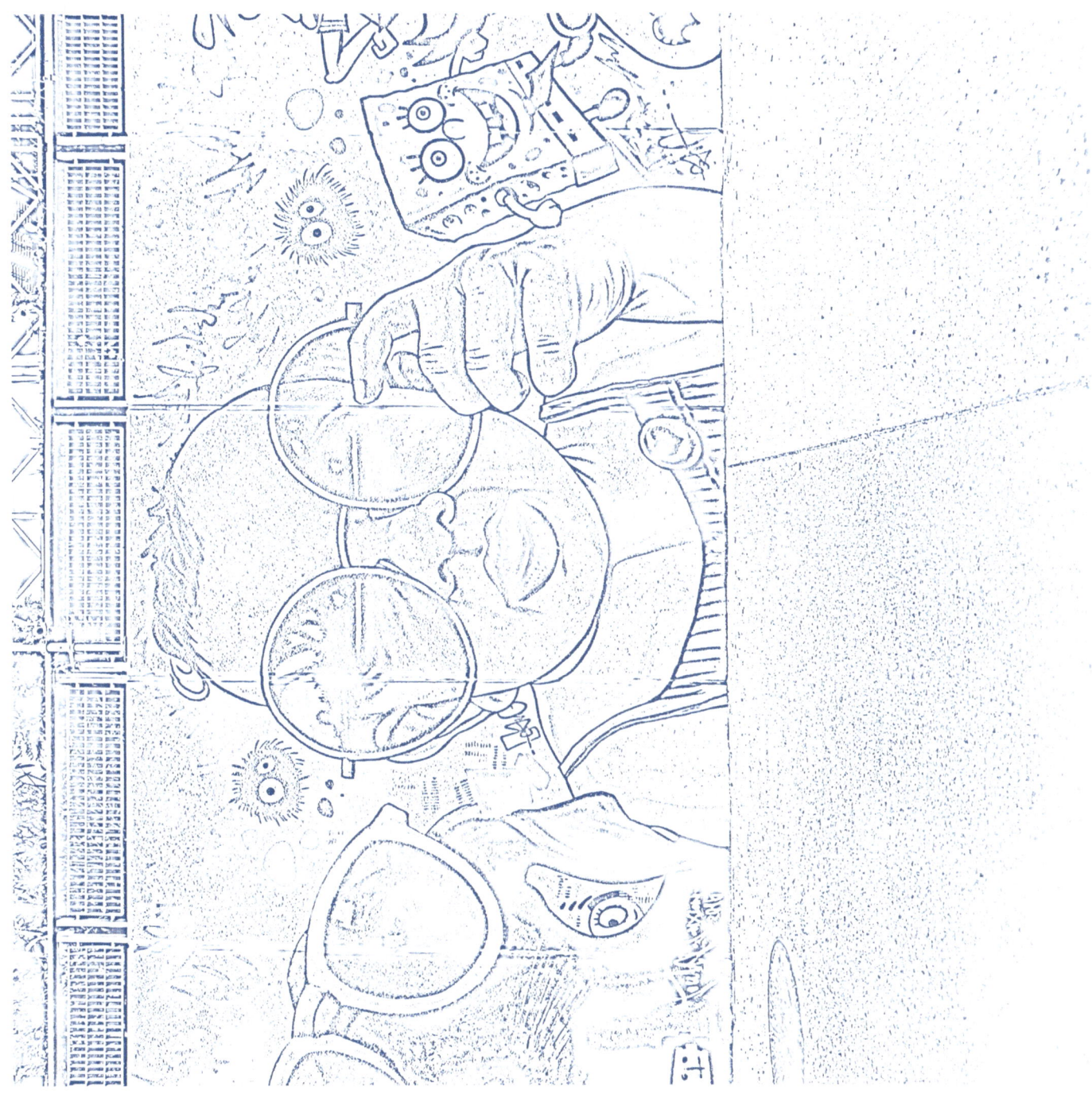

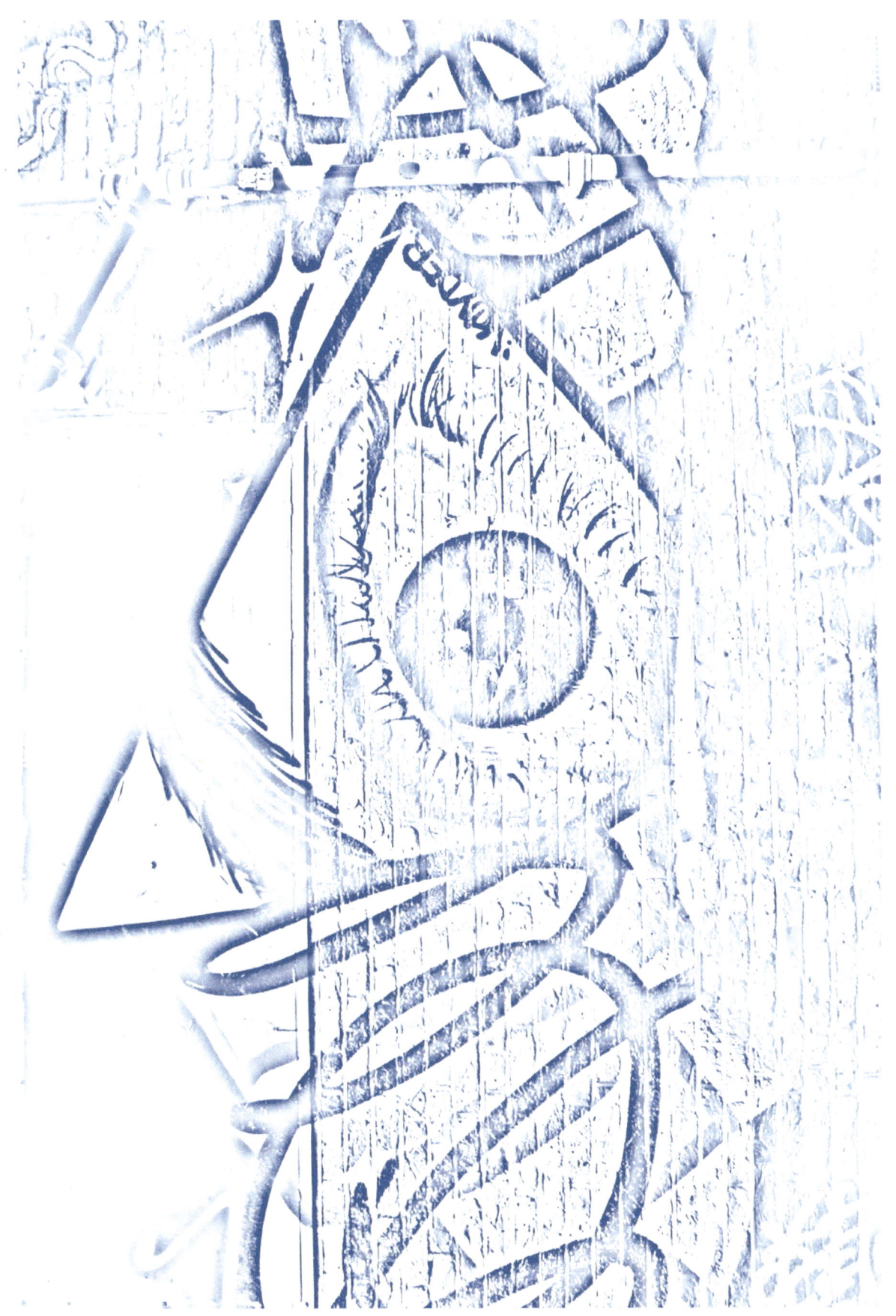

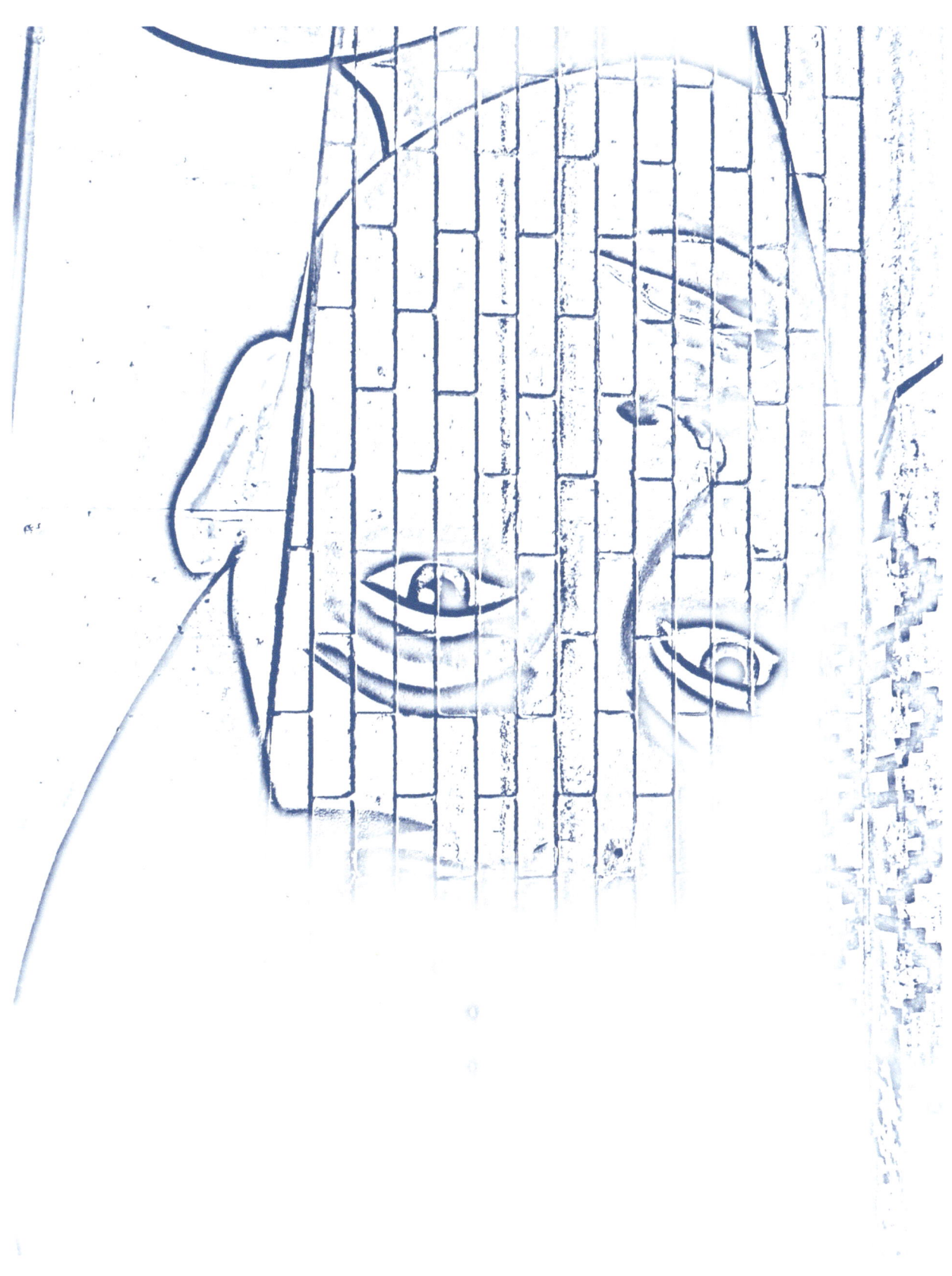

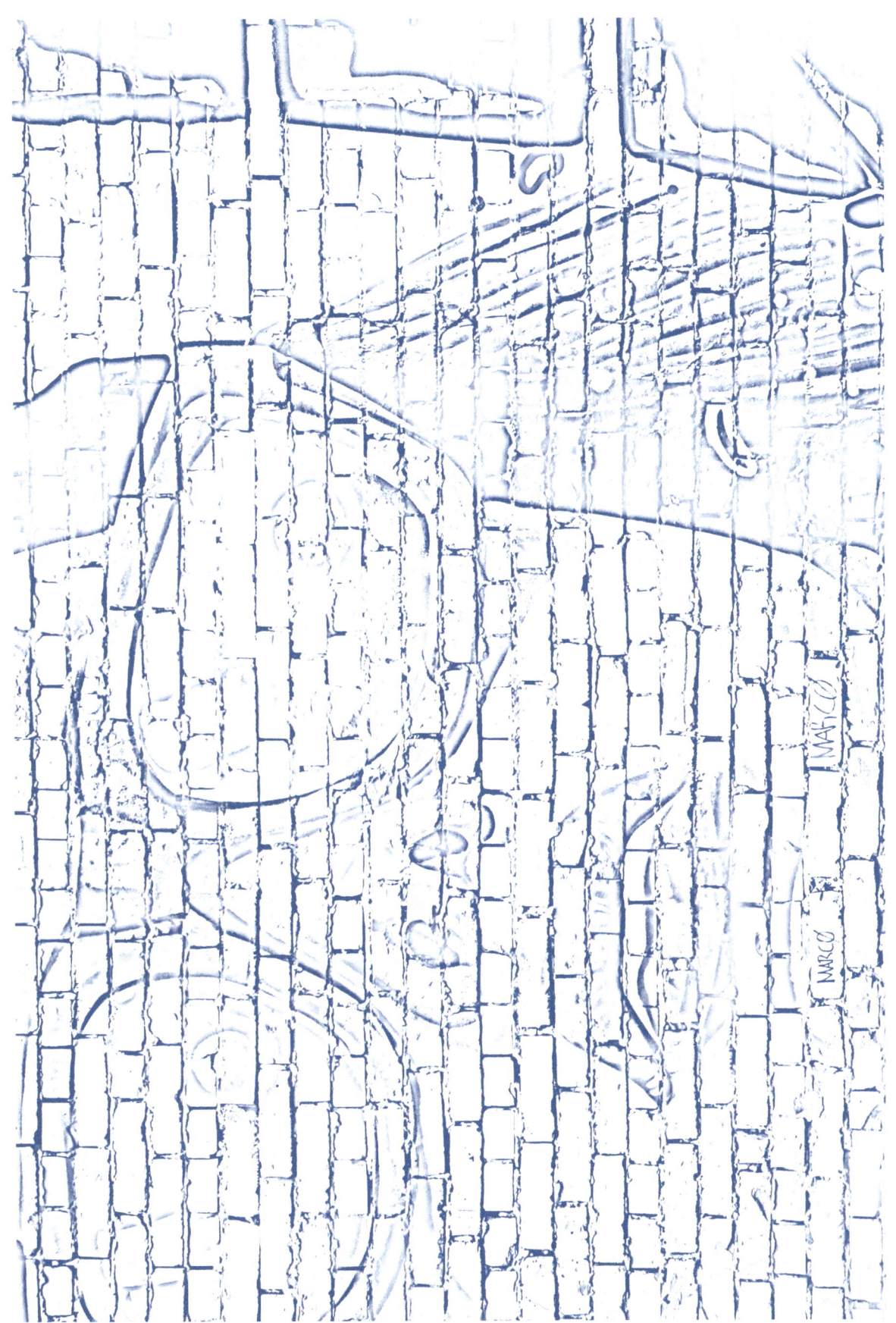

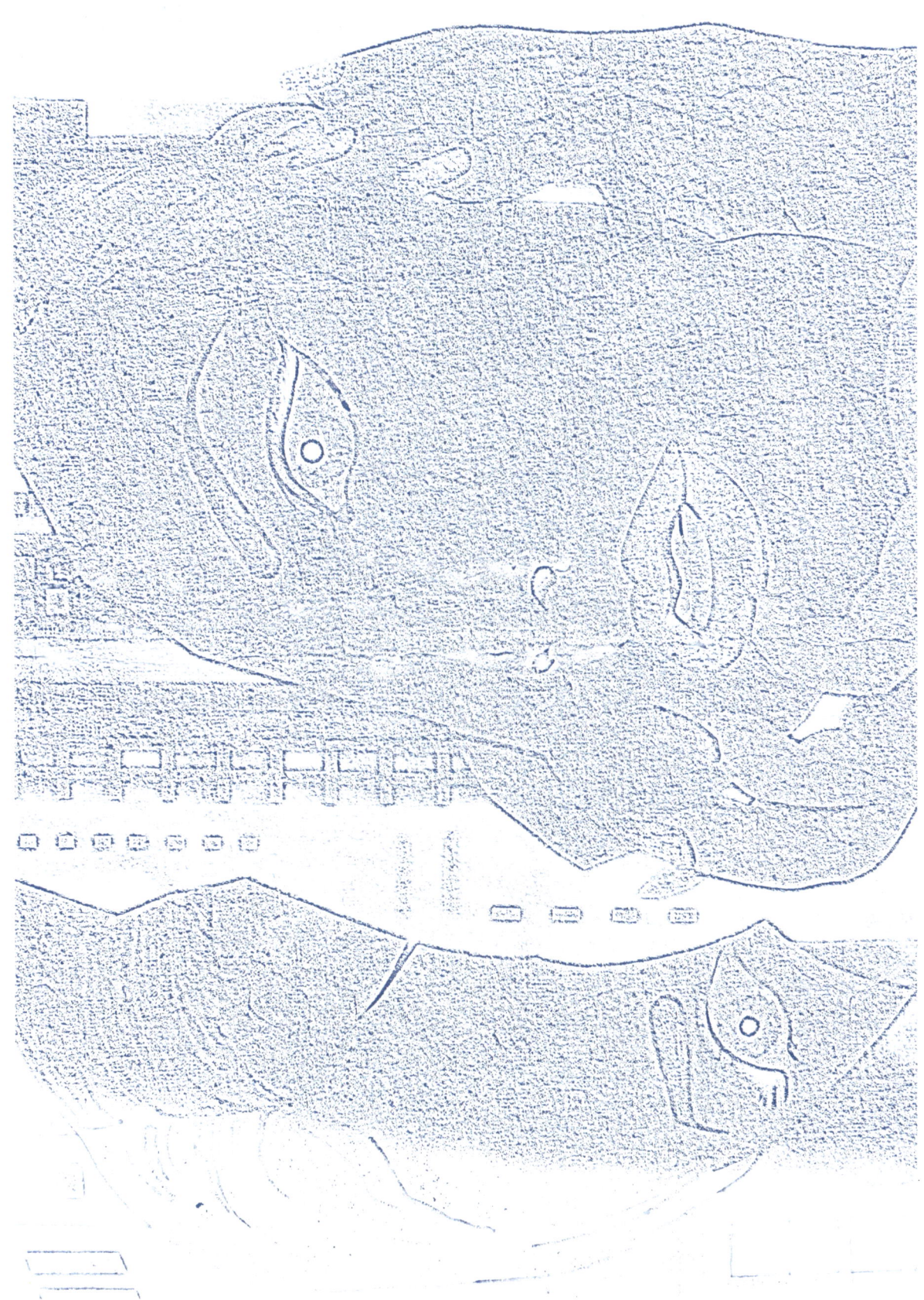

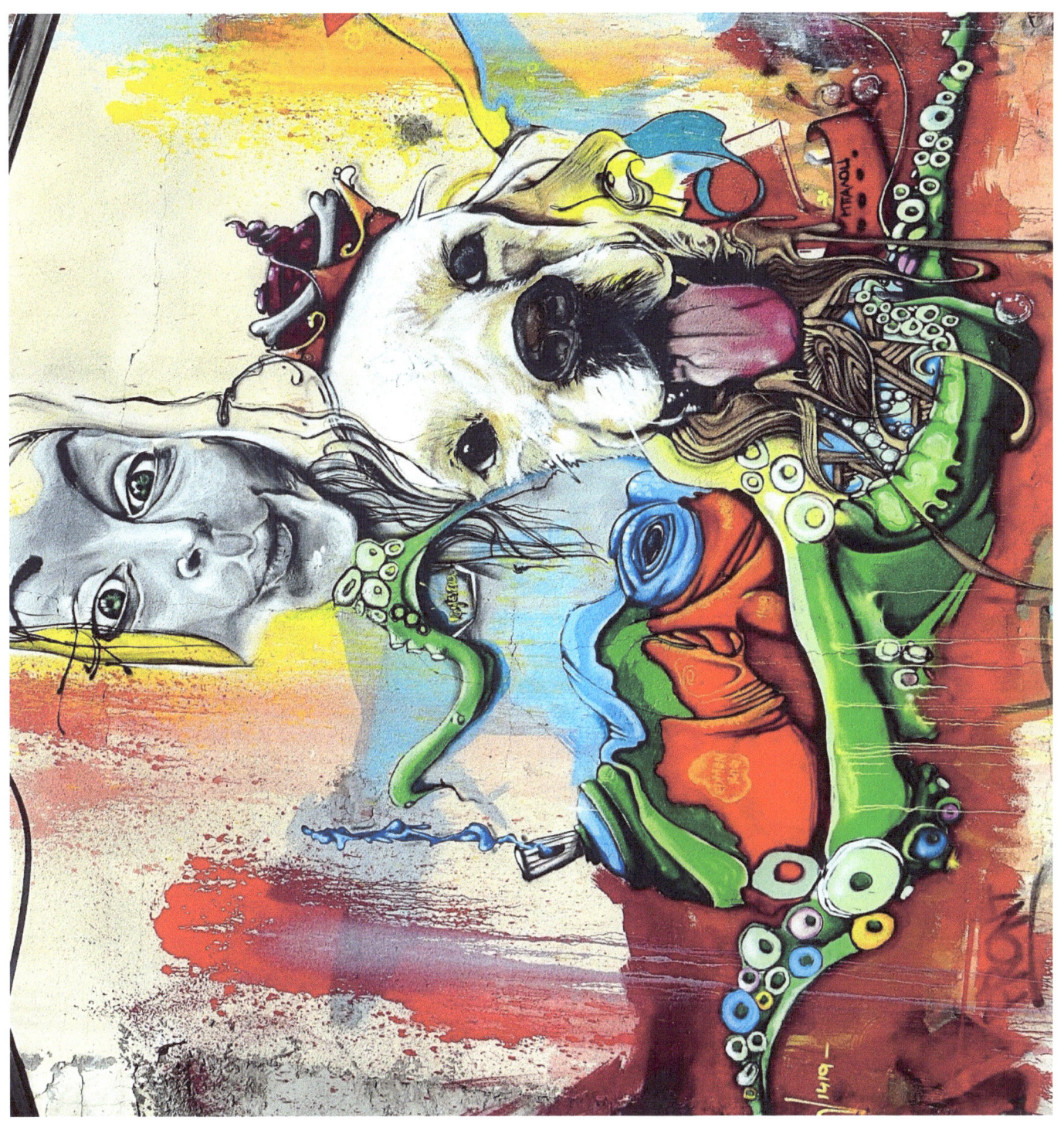

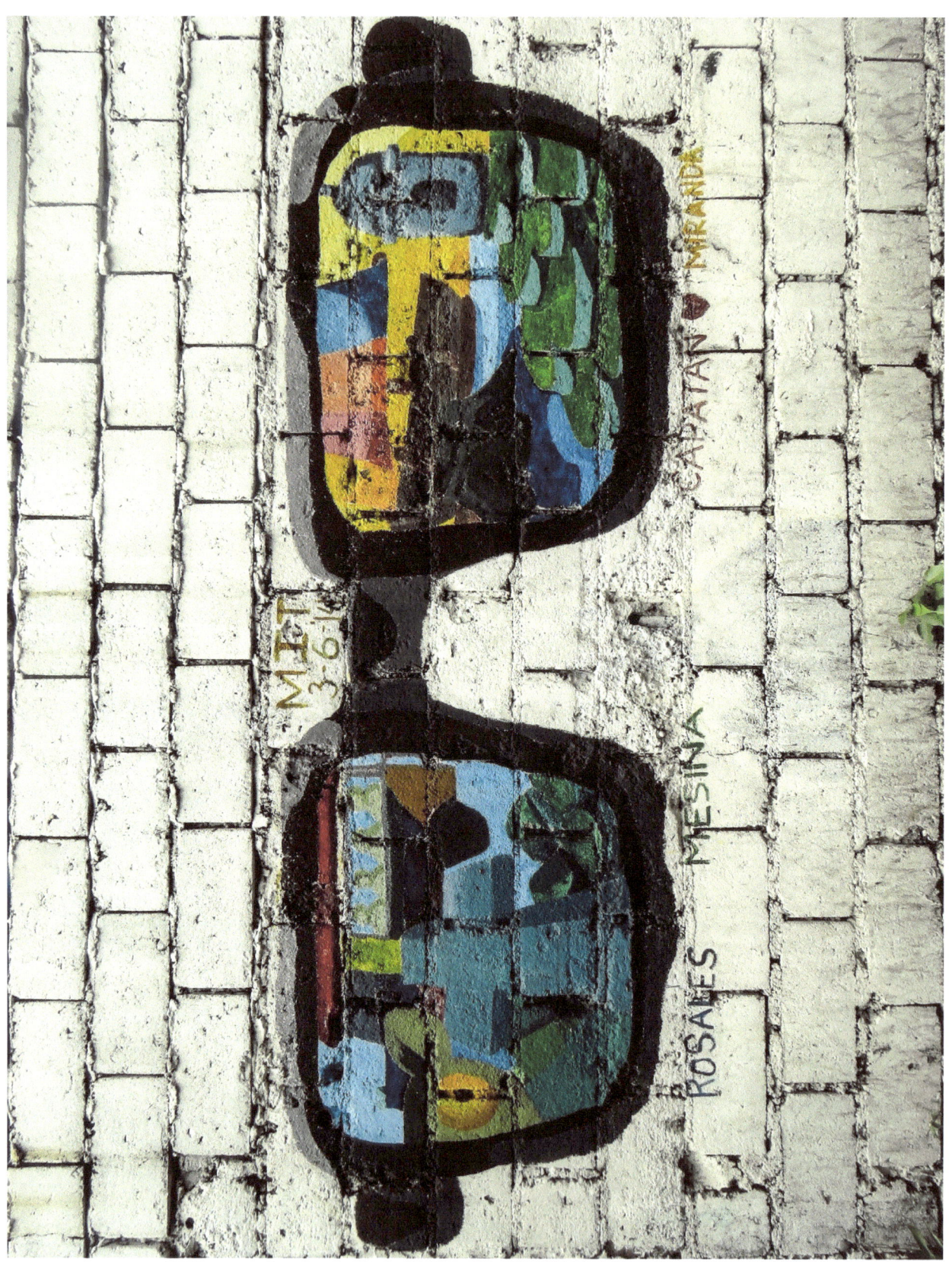

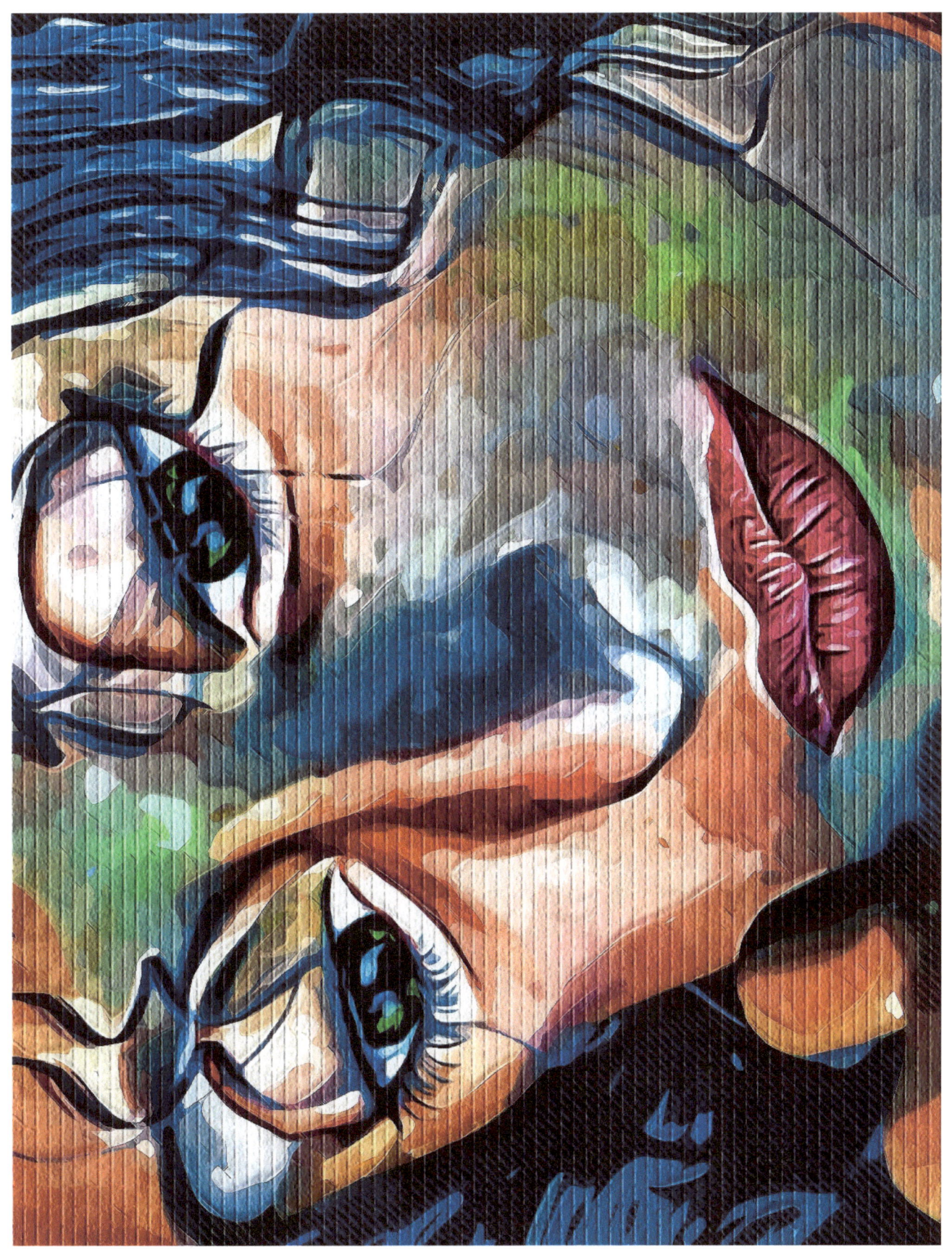

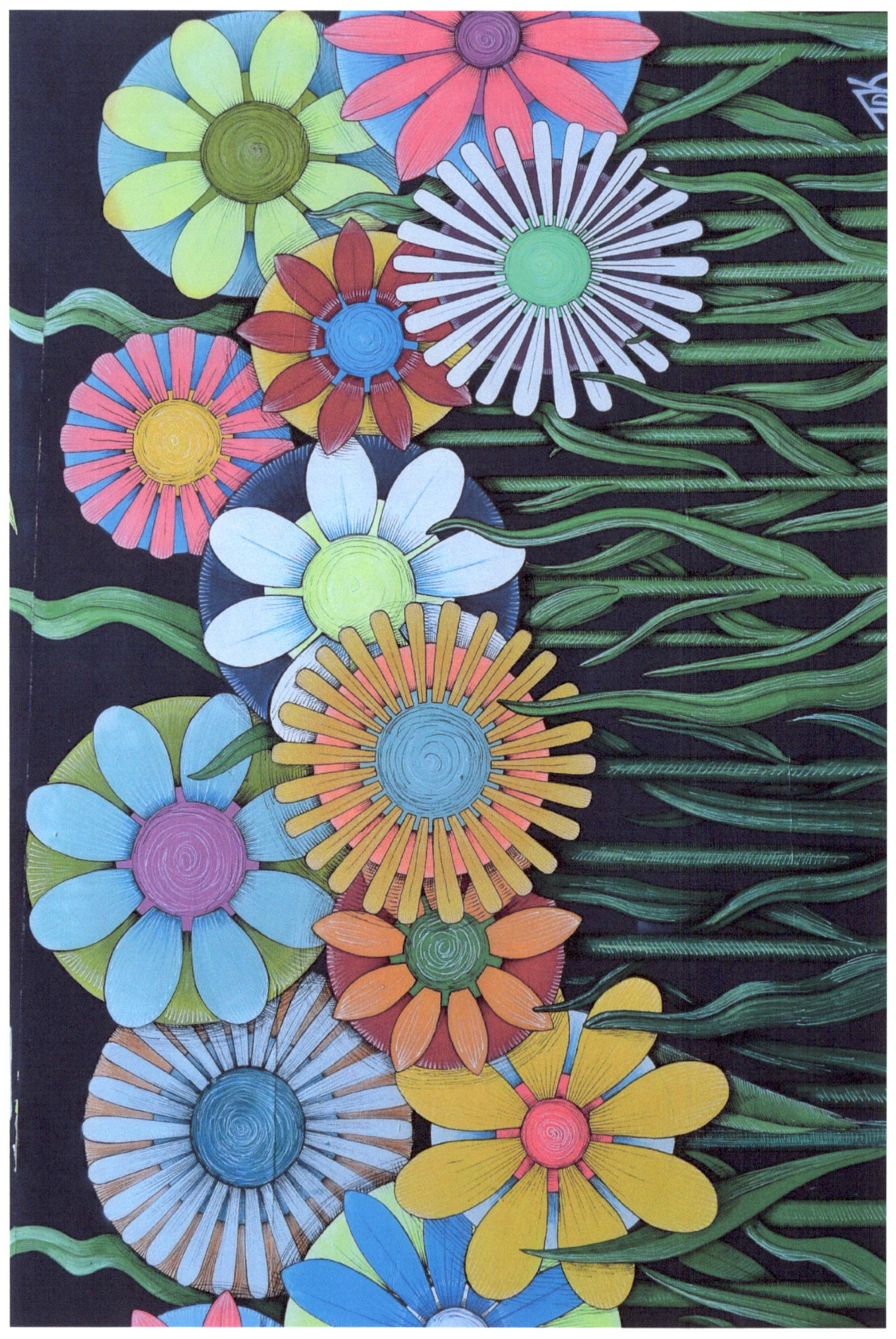

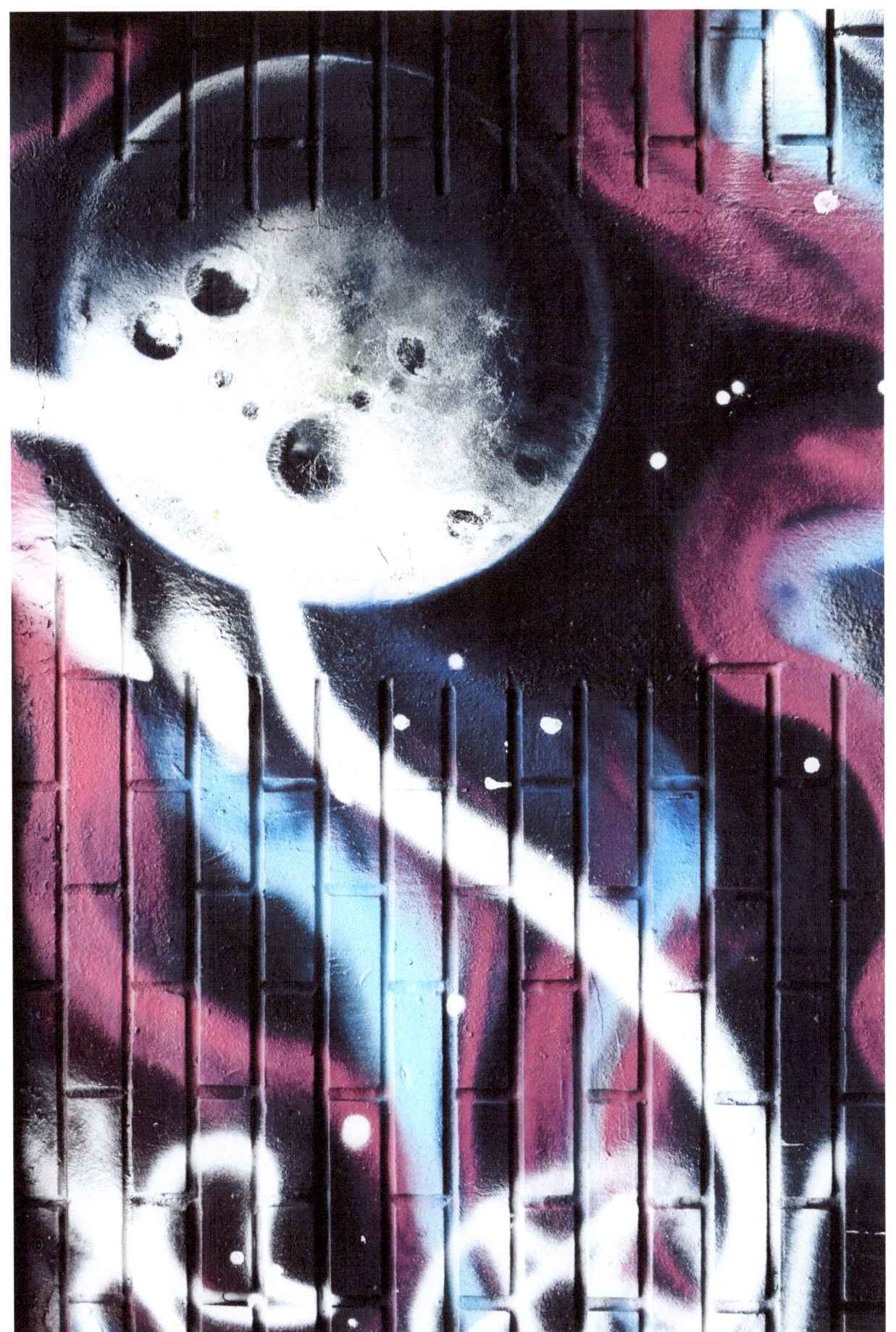

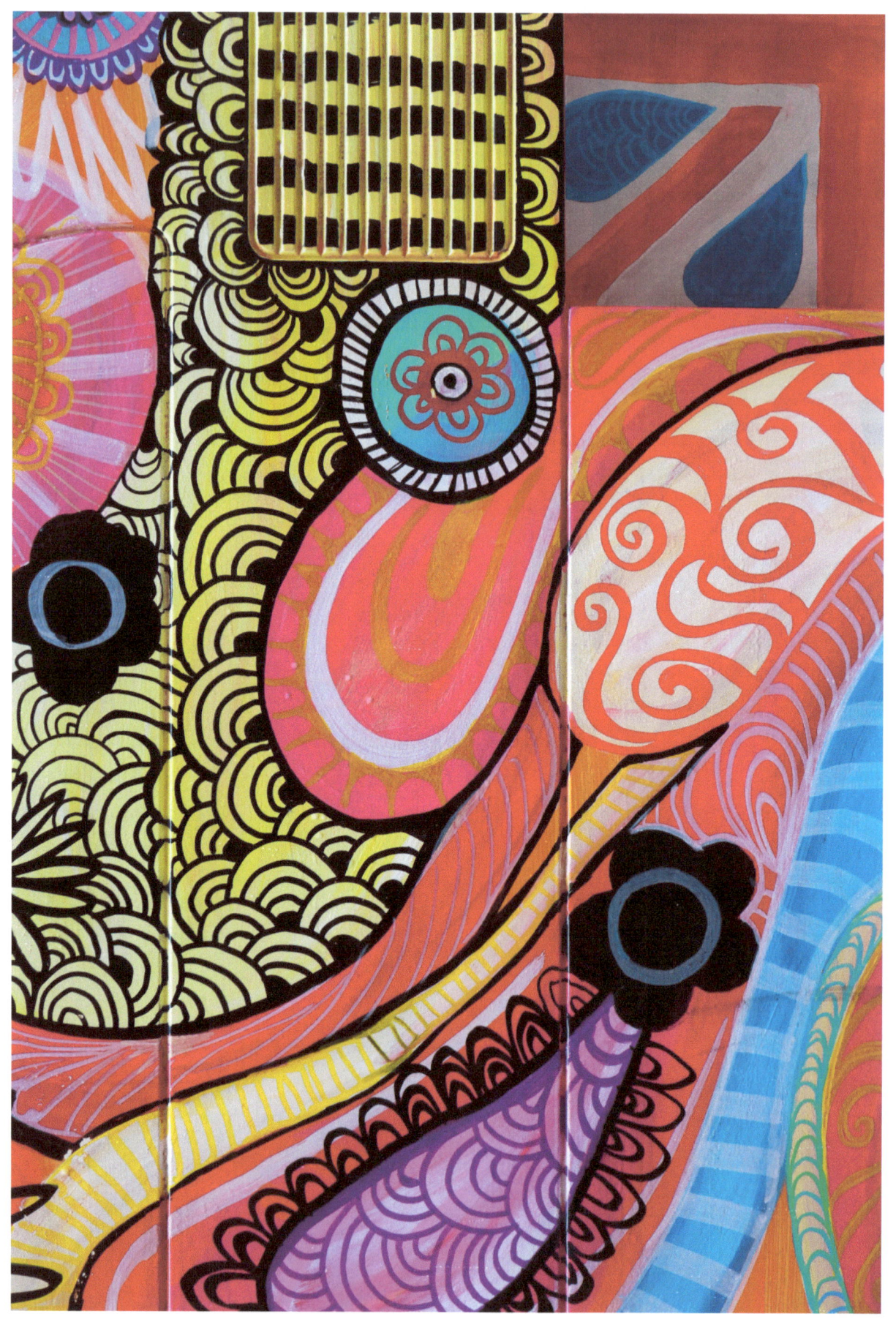

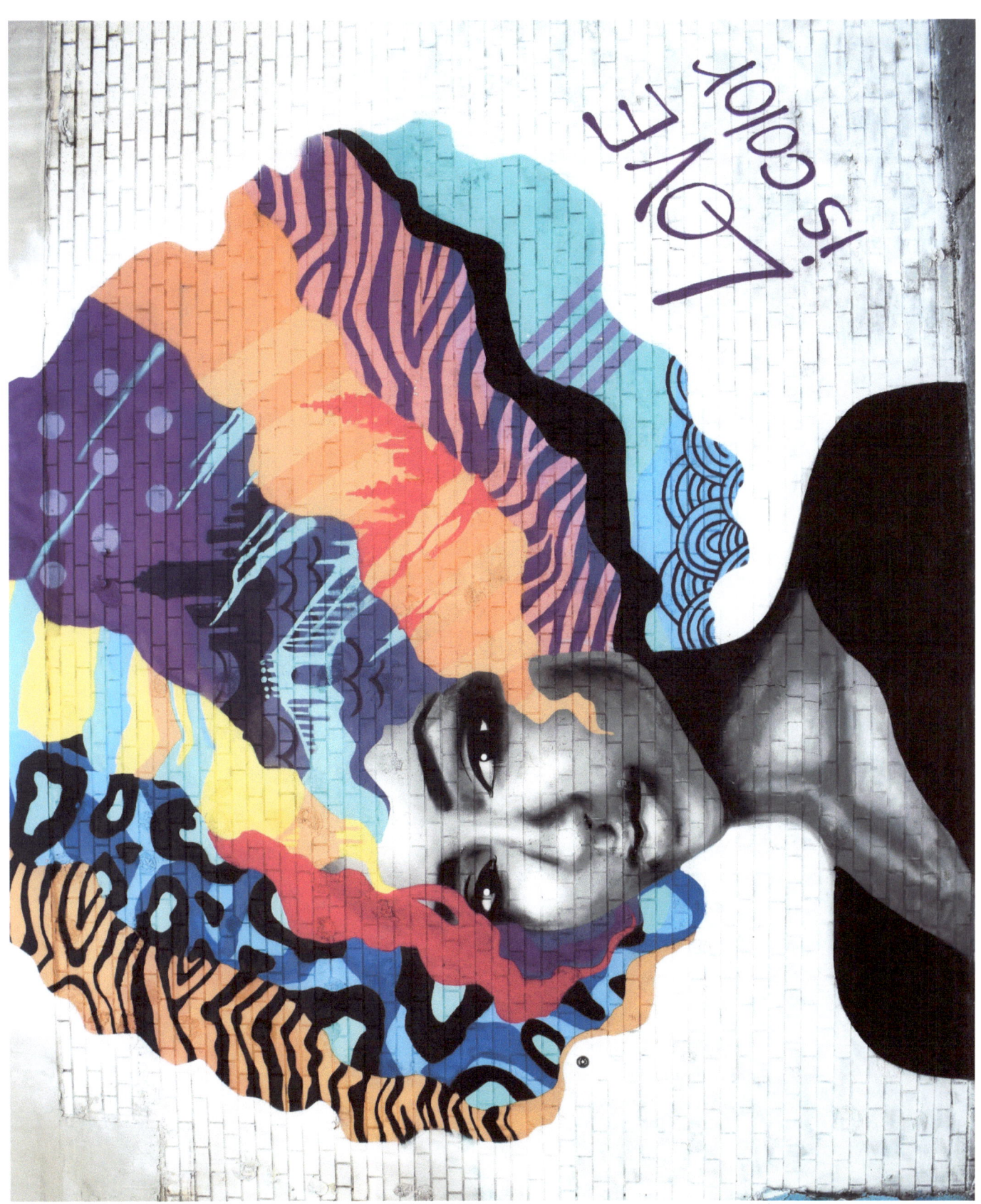

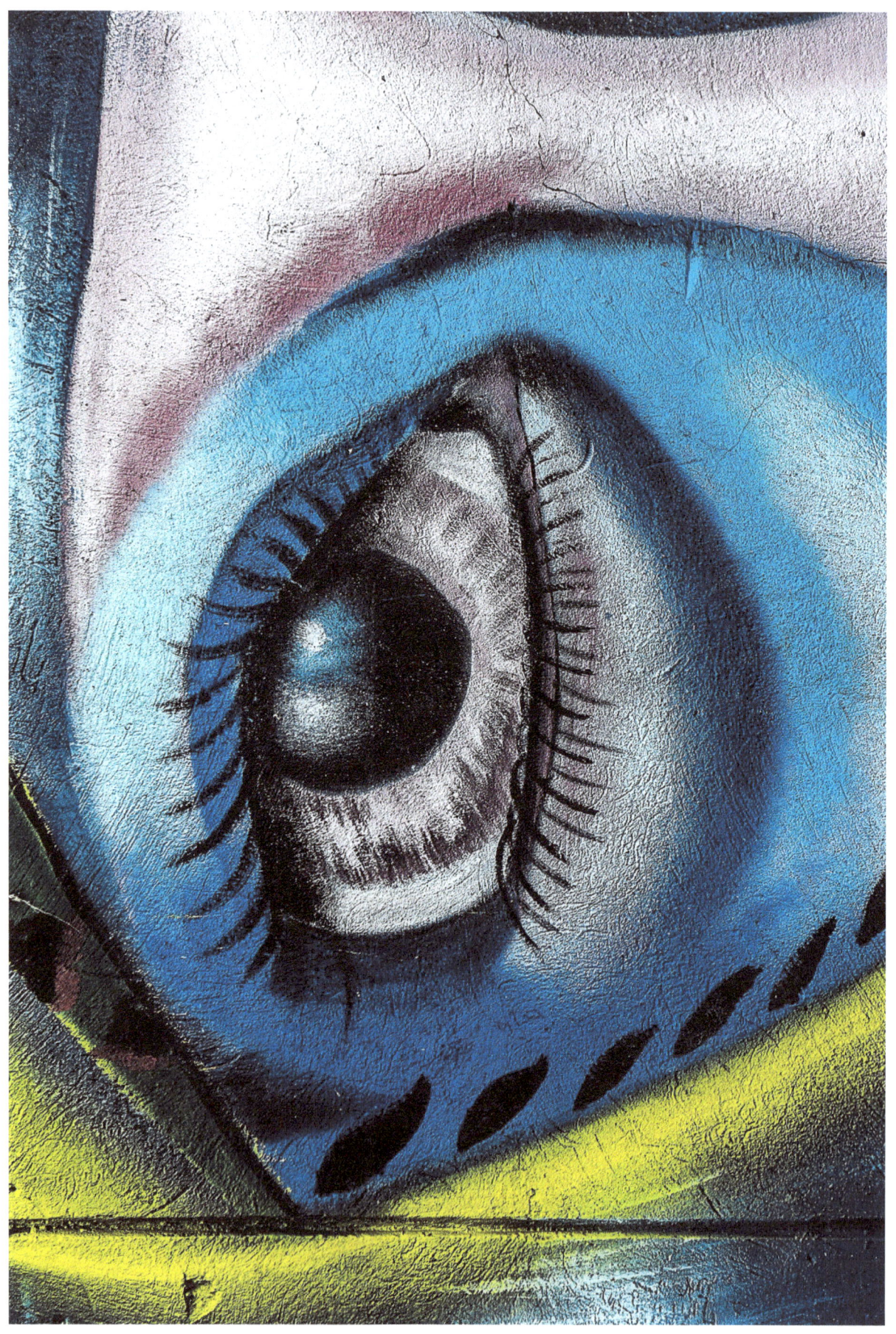

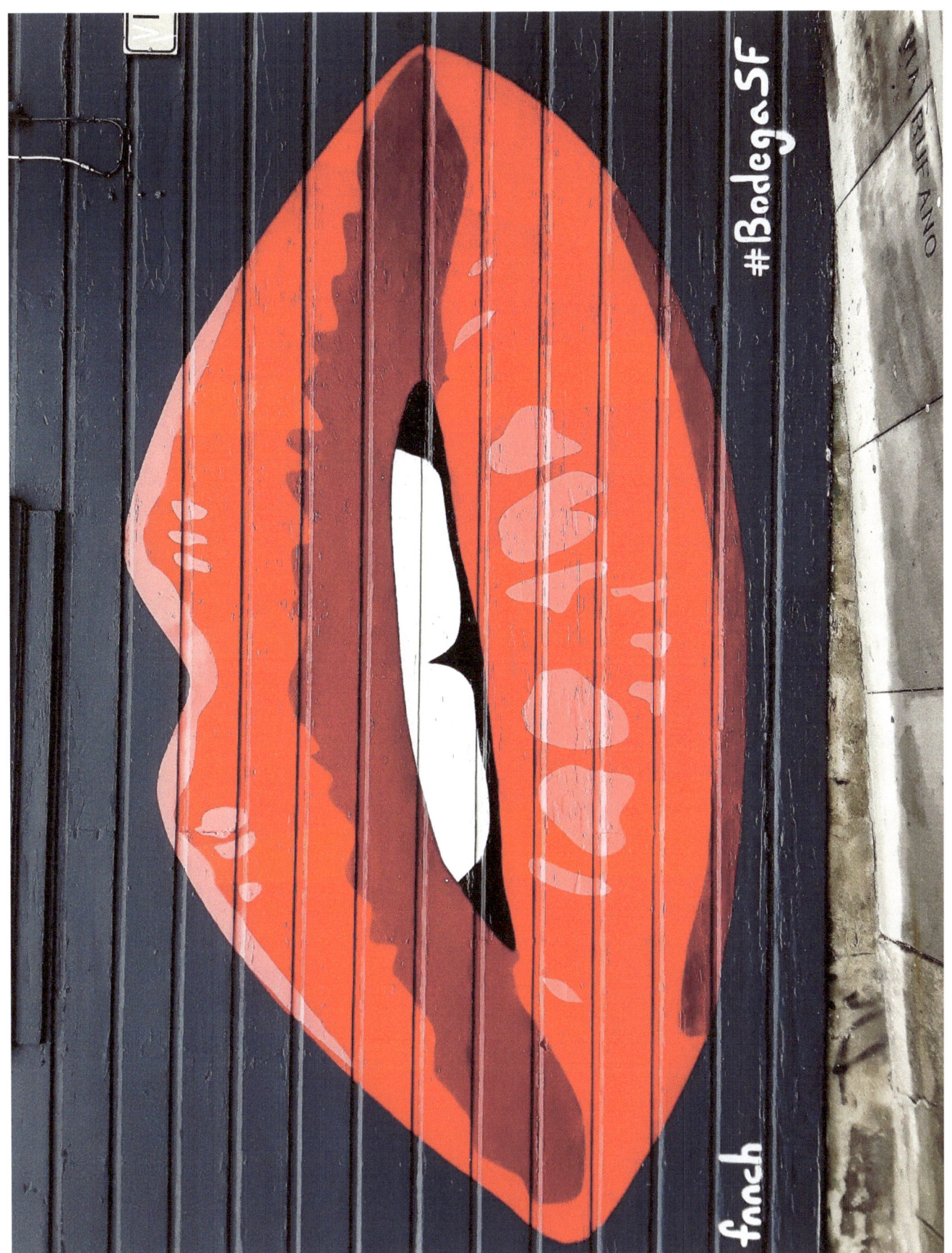

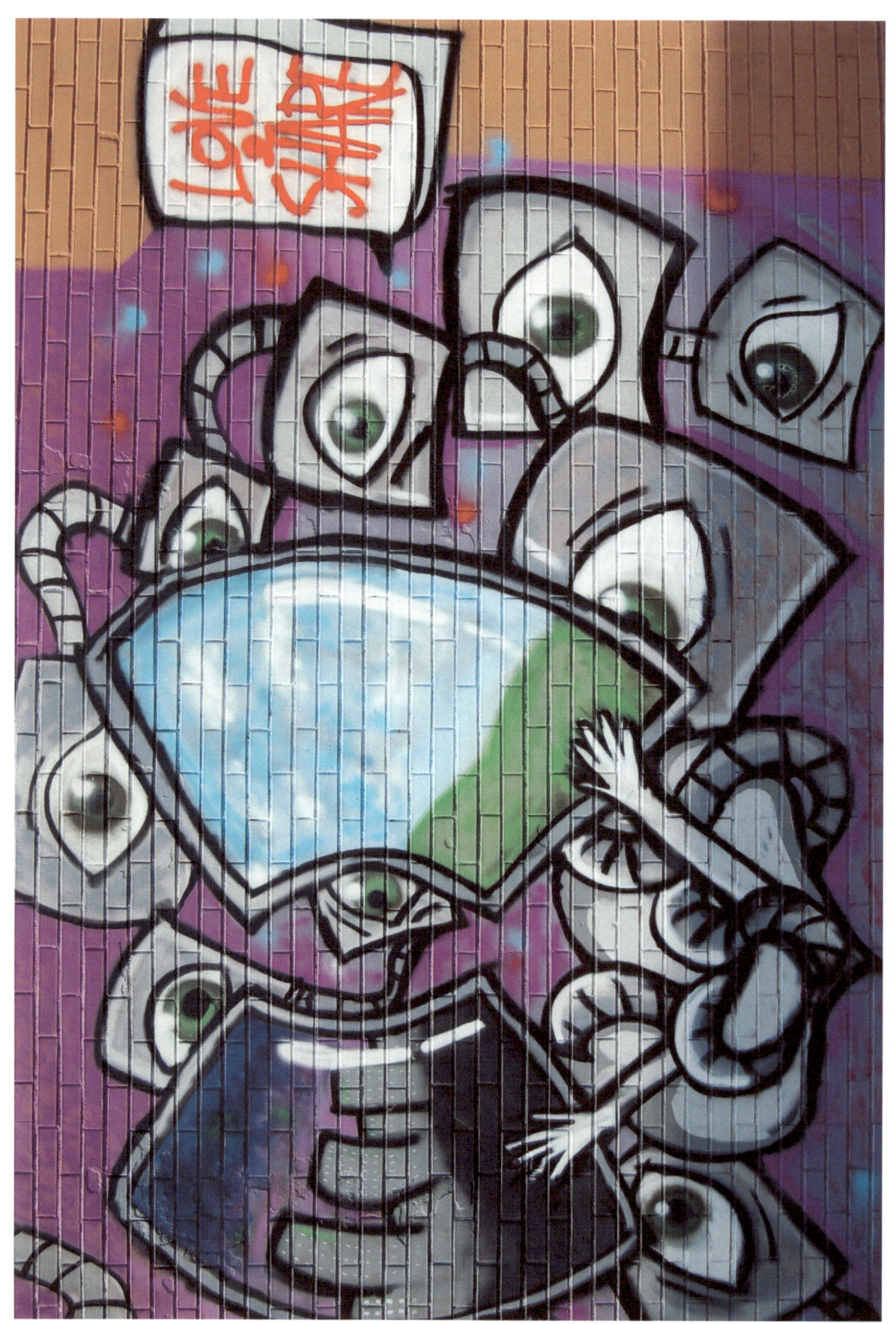

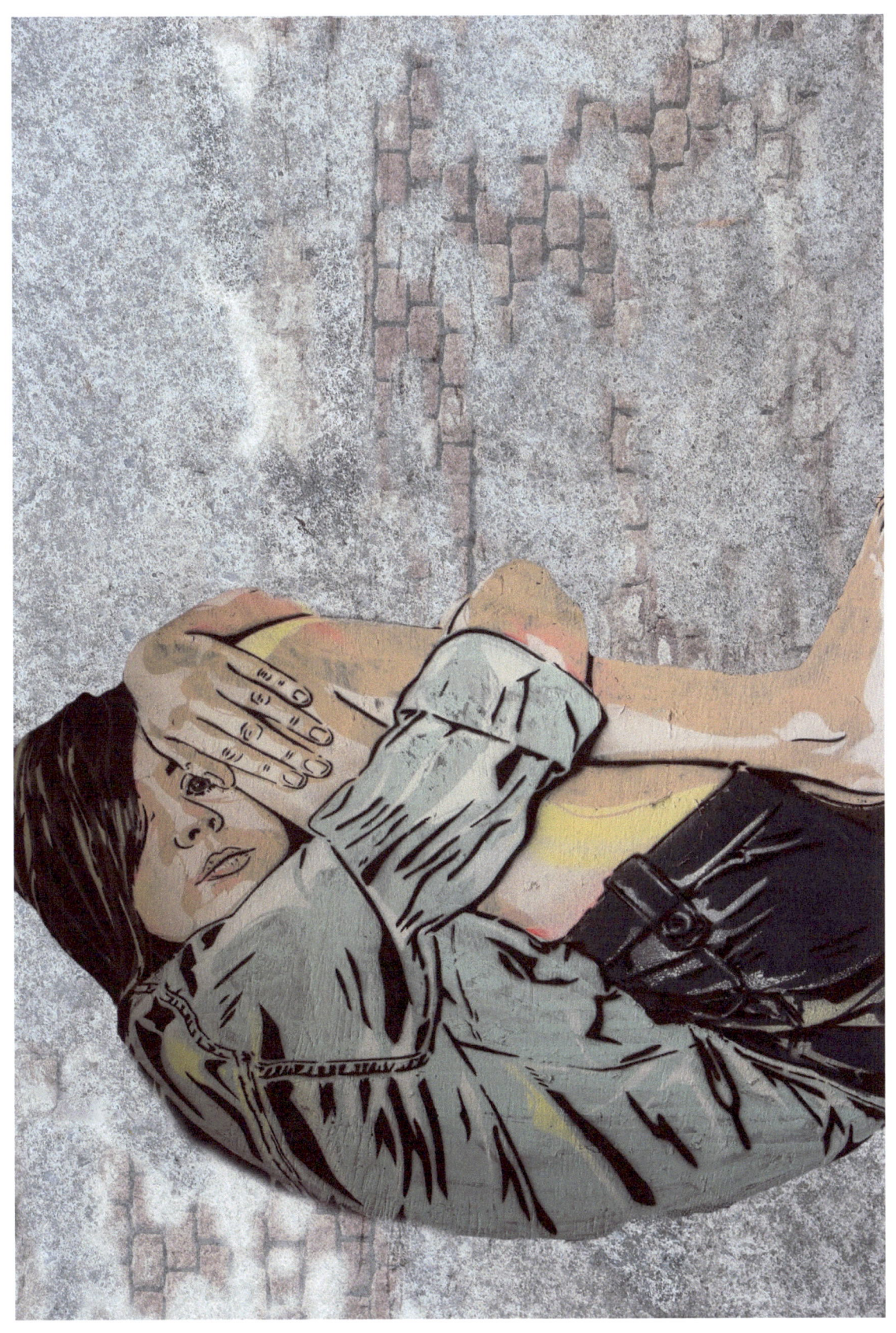

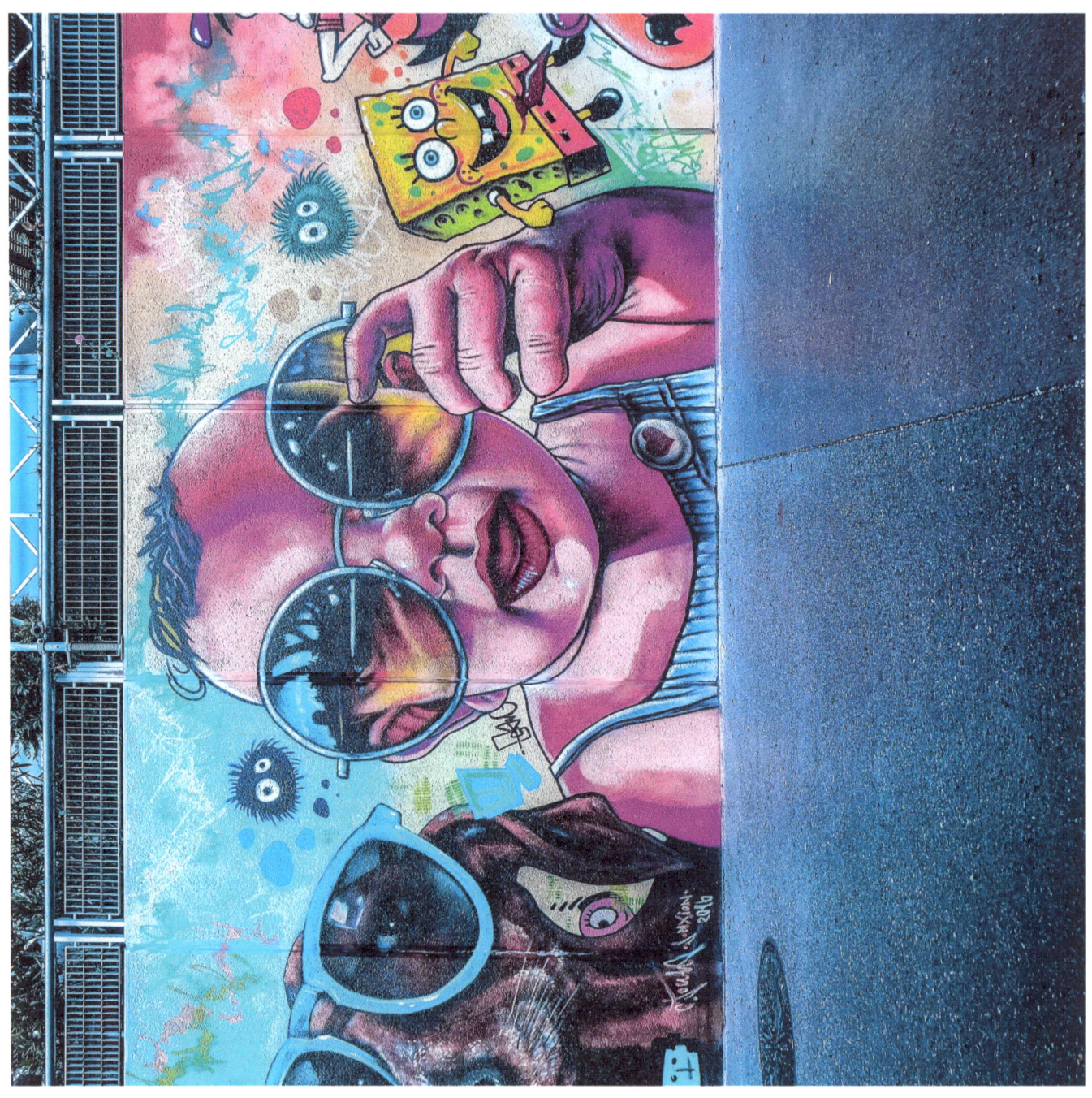

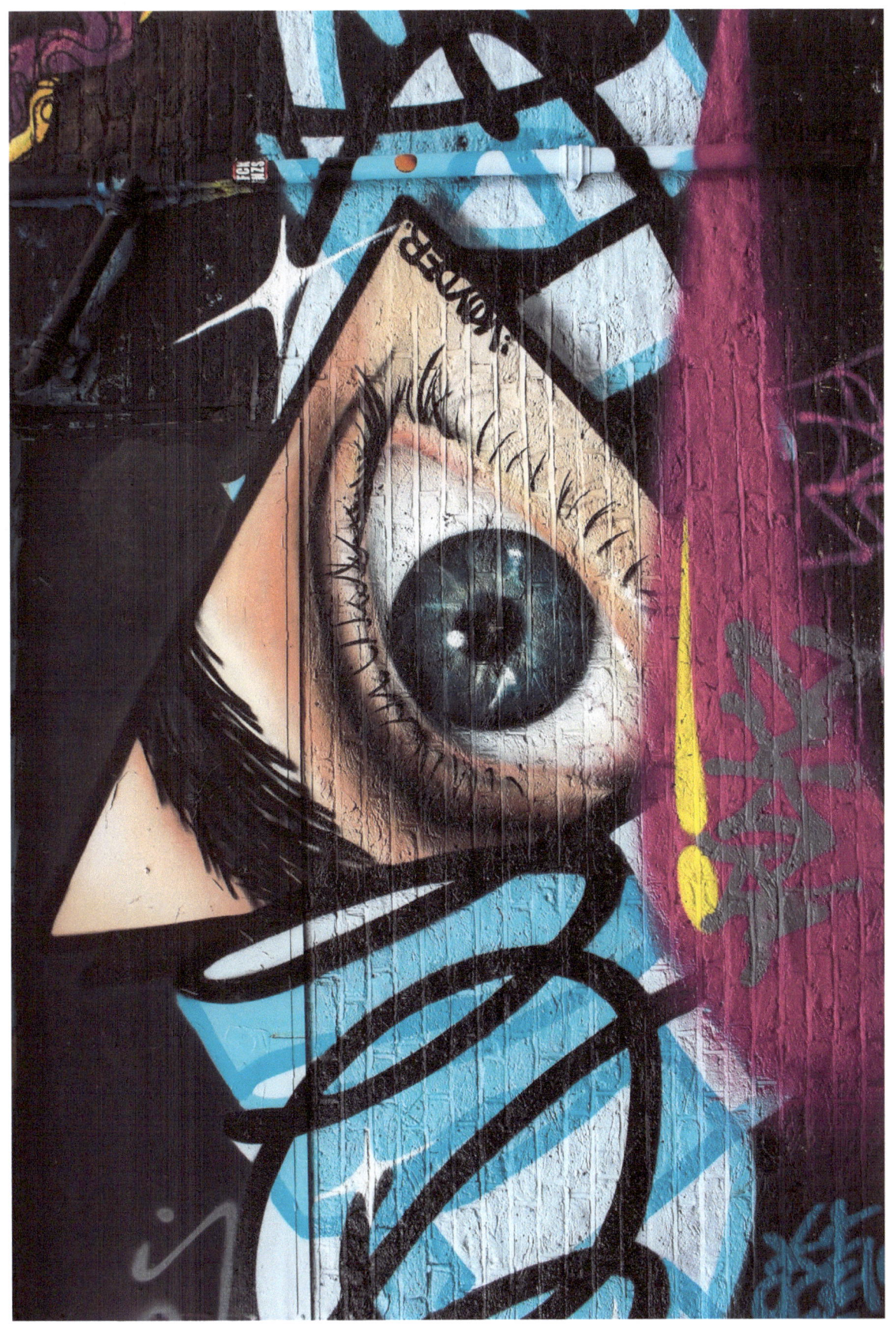

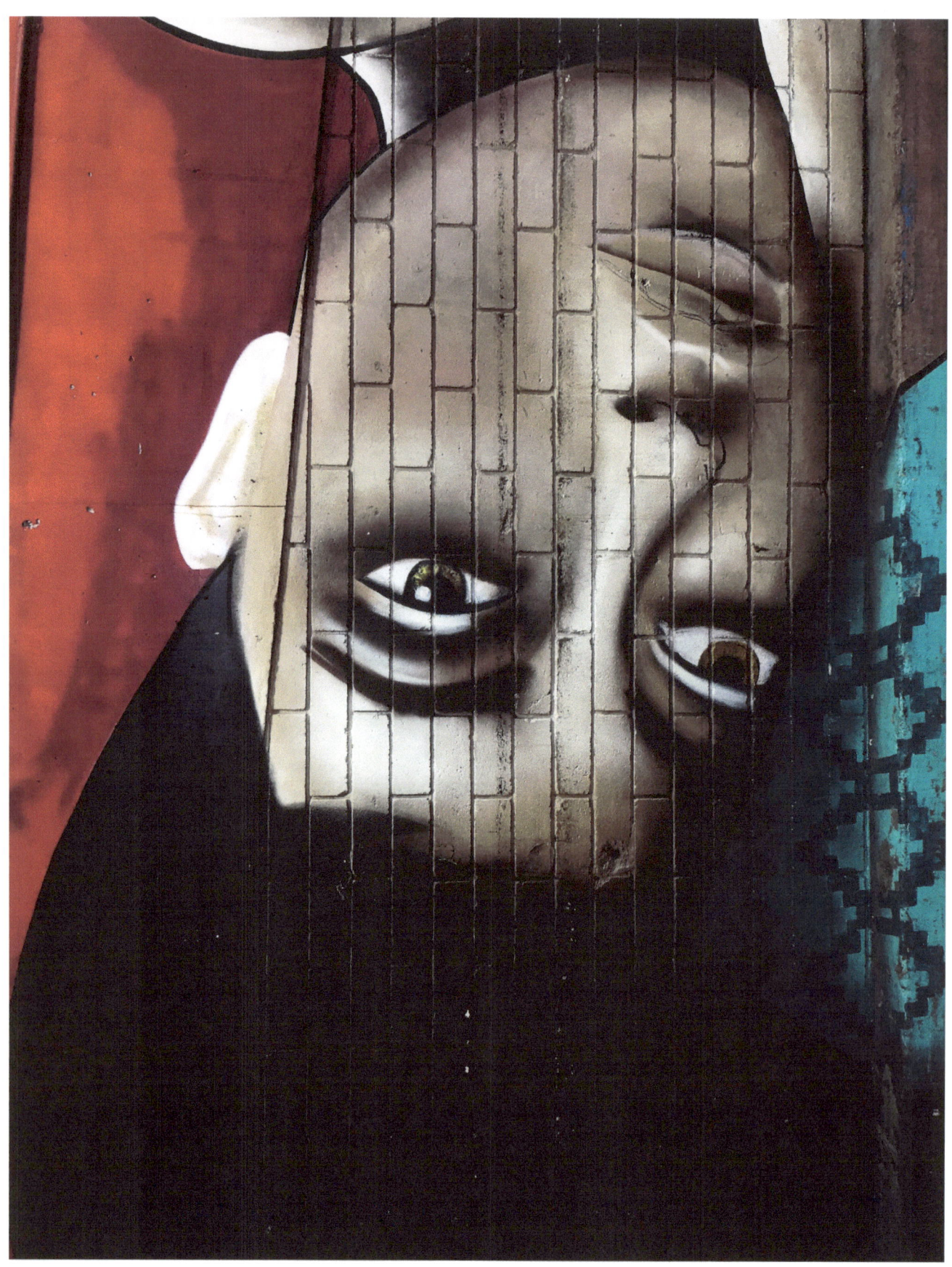

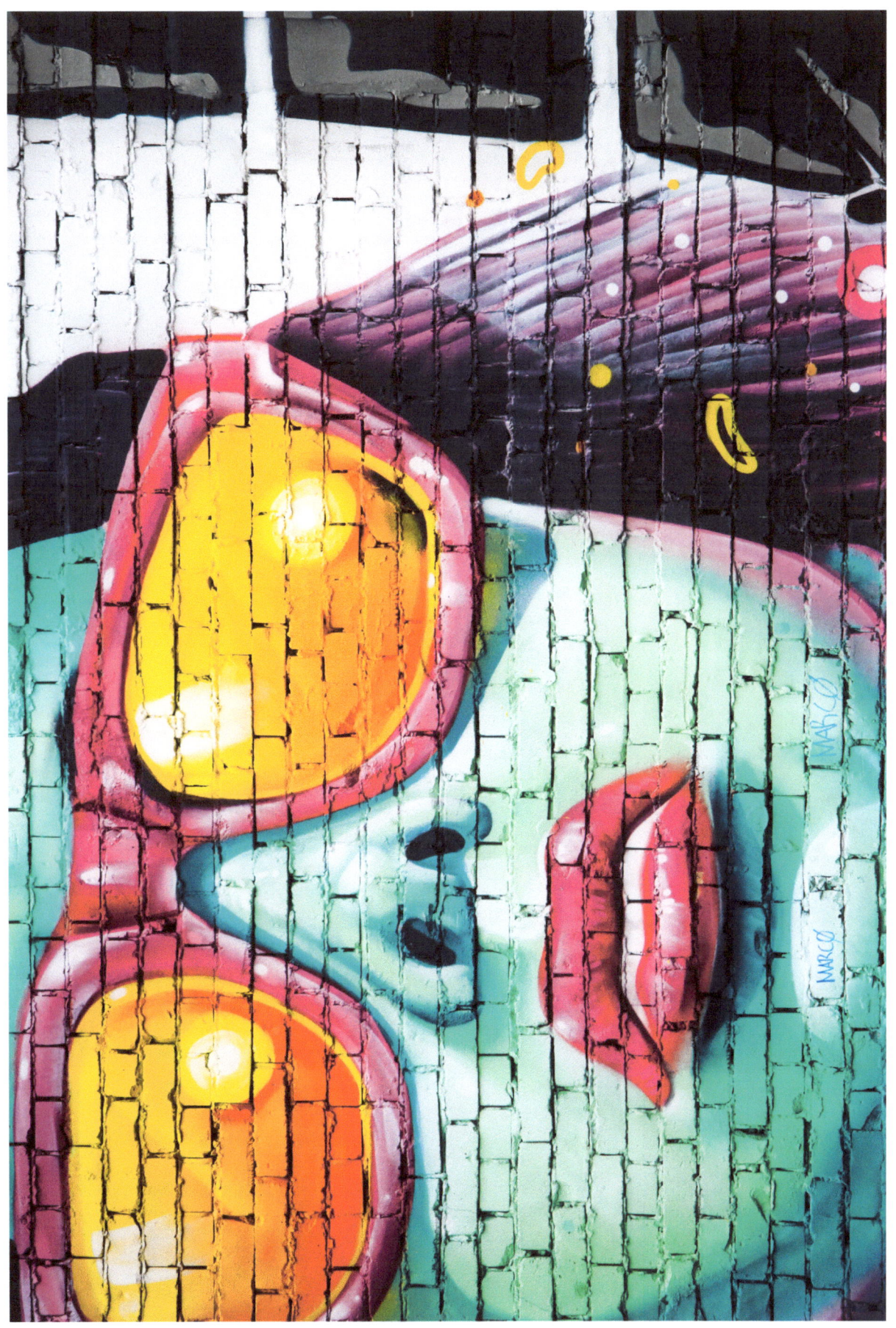

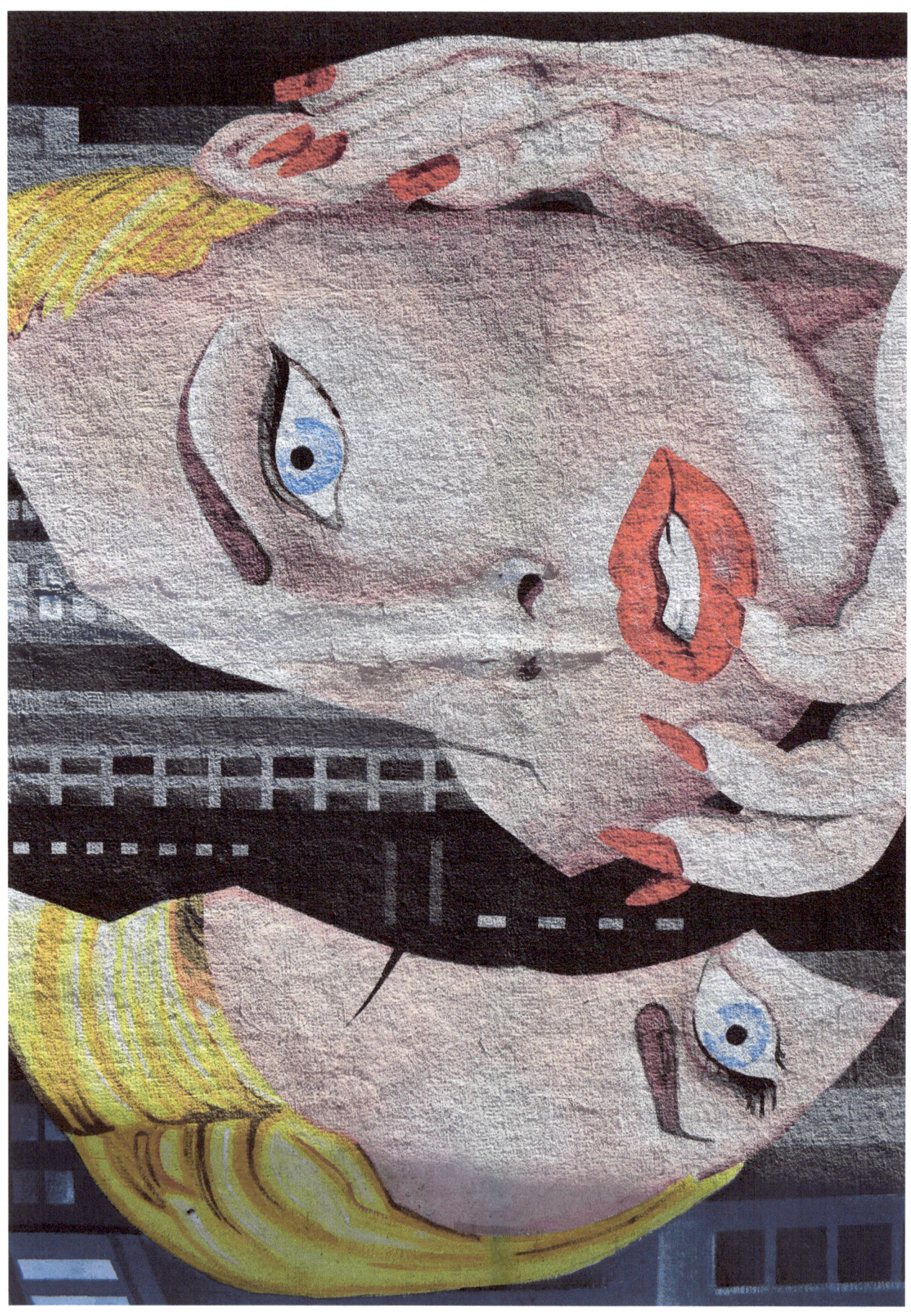